GETTING TO CENTER

ALSO BY MARLEE GRACE

How to Not Always Be Working

GETTING TO CENTER

Pathways to Finding Yourself
Within the Great Unknown

marlee grace

wm

WILLIAM MORROW
An Imprint of HarperCollinsPublishers

GETTING TO CENTER. Copyright © 2020 by Marlee Grace. All rights reserved. Printed in the United States of America. No part of this book may be used or reproduced in any manner whatsoever without written permission except in the case of brief quotations embodied in critical articles and reviews. For information, address HarperCollins Publishers, 195 Broadway, New York, NY 10007.

HarperCollins books may be purchased for educational, business, or sales promotional use. For information, please email the Special Markets Department at SPsales@harpercollins.com.

FIRST EDITION

Designed by Diahann Sturge

Library of Congress Cataloging-in-Publication Data has been applied for.

ISBN 978-0-06-296977-4

20 21 22 23 24   LSC   10 9 8 7 6 5 4 3 2

For Jackie

Who holds her center so well, who is her own

planetarium, the brightest light

CONTENTS

FOREWORD

The first time I saw Marlee was at a hotel lobby for the Decatur Book Festival. She was wearing Blundstones, all-black (very professional), and her hair was in that (iconic) bright, triangular-shaped dirty-blonde bob. I remember thinking her outfit was cute, there was something linear about the lines, the silhouette. I remember thinking that her tattoos were also particularly wonderful. They stood out, reminded me of my own—I'm a Capricorn: shocking no one, *I love my own taste*. Marlee is a Capricorn moon; we simply get each other.

This isn't an understatement. As the months have rolled into countless conversations—as I've fallen in love again, as she moved across the country from Michigan to New Mexico, right through to the outbreak of a pandemic—we've shared moments of deep togetherness, as well as deep parallels between our processes. More than anything, what's become clear is that there's a mirroring between how we both navigate the world.

No big surprise, we have similar traumas. But somehow, miraculously, we've learned how to work through them individually, with an equal amount of compassion and perseverance.

Here's the thing you might not get at first glance: Marlee is spiritually diligent, she's self-aware. I've also come to admire the way she navigates things politically *because* she's diligent—whether it's about queerness, or about being a white woman navigating a white supremacist world, she wants to engage, be curious and she wants to learn. Her responsiveness has felt, at times, a small, and necessary, reprieve.

I've found this most impressively in her writing, in particular this book, which I have been very fortunate to read in its early iterations. In the pages, you'll see someone who is immensely dedicated to the betterment of herself, as she is in the betterment of you. Her enthusiasm is both relatable and revelatory. This is a book made out of love because Marlee loves you. She wants people to be happy, to learn the lessons she's learning herself.

In the pages, as she moves from joy to grief, productivity to rejuvenation—there's an honesty about her own process that makes her words so compelling. There were moments I felt deeply seen, and where a deep-bellied *aha* arose through me because she writes as she speaks to you when she's your friend: She's direct, she's funny and she's honest about how deeply hard work it is to be invested in your own happiness.

As I read the book, I felt moved that I had a friend that would take the time to catalog what she's found works for her. Marlee is the teacher and the student.

There's so much about her that moves me—as a friend, comrade, and colleague—and I've felt deeply blessed by her care as I've struggled these last few months in my own life. In moments of my own darkness and sometimes gloom, she's shown up for me, something I didn't even need to ask her to do. Which is something this book does too: it shows up. Do you have a question on how to proceed on work, life, love? Marlee might have some answers for you!

That's another thing—she quietly leads by example. She *wants* to be a good person, and actively seeks that journey with vigilance, and this book is an example of that work. This is an intimacy that translates into Marlee's artwork, something that's no doubt made her a charming light beam. Marlee's art, like Marlee herself, is expansive, its many dimensions of her being and her thoughtfulness. She spreads herself, like only an adept Gemini would, and brings all of herself to the hopeful bettering of anyone who trusts her. Thing is, she makes you want to trust her. She makes you feel safe too. She makes you want to go on the journey with her, and like she is in real life, she becomes the friend you didn't know you wanted.

EARLIER THIS YEAR, Marlee came and stayed with me. It was January, about a month and a half before Covid-19 would truly hit the US. It feels like ages ago, but we spent a few days cooking, talking, writing alone, watching *Sex Education* in my bed, and going to the Lesbian Herstory Archives in Park Slope. She danced for me, and we blew smoke out the kitchen window. I was just officially falling in love with my now partner, and she guided me through it. Held me as I remembered, completely lovesick, the intensity of falling in love again and what it meant to be so moved by love, unexpectedly. She talked about Jackie, her partner, and there was a feeling of the sincere relief you get when you are able to talk to someone who understands (because they're also in one) queer partnership.

In the time that I've known her, she's made me understand why I saw her in our shared hotel lobby. There's something deeply compelling about the work she has dedicated herself to. As her friend, we talk about it often. About the struggles of being spiritually focused. Just today, I was on the phone with her and we talked about being public and about desirability, and what comes with the intensely introjected fear of one's inherent unlovability . . . and how that clashes when you're being "seen." With this book, she'll go there with you, to those depths.

It's a tough job to be a vessel. Especially one without ego—that's part of the process too, of paring back the bullshit and being faced with who we really are. Marlee does that. She makes it feel safe for you to do it too. I am grateful for her work. To be a witness. This book will remind you of that too, of how lucky we all are to have one another. And how important it is to heal, for ourselves, but also for one another.

Love from Under the Corona Sun,
March 2020
Fariha Róisín

INTRODUCTION

Believing in ourselves is not a task or a chore of ease, unless we make it so. While mental health and self-worth are not always pathways of choice, we can build this into our practice. Choice making as re-centering. Re-centering as choice making.

This is the beginning. We'll talk about beginnings together. And endings. Because everything that ends has a beginning, and everything that begins will end. This is the beauty! Of the process! Of getting to center.

I'd like to start out with what "center" even is. Part of the experience of reading this book will be that you get to define it for yourself. However I'd like to also share what my experience has been with defining my own center.

Instead of "finding balance," I like the language of "getting back on the beam." As if to say, we will always get knocked off, and we may get knocked off when we least expect it. You might picture the beam where gymnasts do amazing tricks. They flip and spin through the air, and then, with a mix of luck and skill, they stick the landing in their sparkly leotards and throw their hands up. You know the move. So I've built tools into my life that help me get back on the beam faster. We're going to build those tools so we perform that move with more ease. And if we don't stick the landing and instead break both ankles and crumple into a ball, we're going to figure out how the hell to start over again.

Another important point I want to make is that you are not the center. You contain a self-defined center, but you as a soul-holding, breathing person are not the center. And we should all be so lucky to both give up this ego-driven placement in the world as well as feel a sense of freedom—to be relieved of this great responsibility is a gift.

In these pages, we are not going to try to solve anything, or to find great and restorative balance. Because if there is one thing I know from creating this book and this life of mine, it is that almost nothing makes sense. Or, that it all makes sense in the perfect and divine path that is your aliveness. Or, that nothing is out of place; everything is on time. Or, that no matter how many times you get far away from your truth, there will always be a path to get back to it. Or to carve out a new one. Or to literally destroy every path ever, because all the paths sucked, and now you need a new path that no one has ever created before.

Your bones and your muscles and your heart hold everything you've ever dreamed of. Ever dreamed up. Ever dreamed about. You can have the life you want, even if you don't think you deserve it.

I write to you from a place of expansion. I leave my smallness behind in these pages not because I believe I am not small, but because I WANT to believe I am not small. Because I want to believe in my fullness, and I want to believe in it because I want you to believe in yours.

Getting to Center emerges from me as a personal offering. I am not an anthropologist or a therapist or trained in any type of advice giving. This is not an advice book. This is the way I do life, the ways I find myself over and over again, a tornado person's anthology of being. It is my way of saying: *Hello, I've tried a few things, now let me tell you how, and maybe you could apply a piece of this to yourself.*

I am a dancer, first and foremost. An improviser, a studier of choice making and compositional practice. This is my entry point for everything I do. I look at the big picture and ask what is needed. What can be added? What can be removed? What if I did the same thing over and over and over again until it made sense, and what if I let that be okay?

In my thirty-two years on Earth, I have begun and ended many things. Sometimes on purpose and on my own terms, sometimes on other people's terms. This is a glimpse into what that experience has been like for me. Through the eyes of my queerness, my sobriety, my miraculous time on Earth. As with anything I share, it is also through the lens of my privilege, my whiteness, and my cisgendered and abled body. A body that holds tangible and emotional pain. A body and a heart and a mind that are learning how to be in the world and grow out of my smallness—for the benefit of all of us.

May your experience with this be fruitful. May you hate certain parts, and may those parts challenge you to develop your own brilliant modalities that suit you perfectly. May the parts that inspire you keep you alive for one more day, keep you hopeful and connected to your body. May your body be healthy and strong, and may those barometers be set by you and only you. I see you; I'm with you. I write this to be less alone in my own mind, to connect with you in this vast performance piece that is reality, that is our forever returning to self and center and abundance. In less scarcity and more—there is enough. Let this prayer ring true.

Throughout this book, I will refer to my partner, the partner I had while I wrote this book. Jackie holds her own center so well, so that I may be my own planetarium with my own center. I will talk about the home in Michigan I wrote most of this in, and the moves that come after. I will talk about my present experience in the world. About getting and staying sober. And just like everything, by the time you hold this book the places and the people and the facts might be different. But this wouldn't be a true book if I kept the details of my day-to-day life out of its pages. This is a true book because it is true today. And if the facts are different by the time it exists in physical form, it will still have been the truth.

At the end of this book is a list of gratitudes and acknowledgments—but one I wanted to nod to before we begin is the book *Centering* by M. C. Richards. The language of this book has greatly influenced the way I look at my own inner landscape—making meaning in my life and creative work by looking at it as a centering practice.

Richards offers us two concepts that I weave into the pages of this book:

CENTERING AS DIALOGUE

and

CENTERING AS TRANSFORMATION

I'd also like to note the importance of DECENTERING ourselves in situations where it is more generous to step back. To not have a say, to give space to communities or individuals who are asking for it. To me, getting to our own centers gives us more clarity in how to decenter ourselves, whether that is in conversations pertaining to race, class, privilege, or humanness, in any way. We must also find the ways where we are not the center. This book is not about becoming the center, but understanding that we are a tiny part in the vast universe where the center lies. That getting to our own center allows us to see our own humanity with humility and grace, making adequate space for ourselves, and spaciousness for everyone else.

May these small notions carry you through, in whatever you do. Writing this was my own act of devotion, reading my own words was my own act of remembering, and knowing you're reading them is my own act of joy.

Some of this book is how I moved back to Michigan from California to look at the shadow side of myself. To look at what had gone ignored for too long. I am not saying you have to leave your life behind and return to your hometown for eight months to do your shadow work. But I did. I had to do something extreme. I had to remove myself from all social and environmental distractions to truly look at what was underneath—a great discomfort. A fear of success. Disillusionment about self. And an obsession with thinking that something external could solve all of my inner turmoil. *If only I got this opportunity . . . When I find the right love . . .* I already knew alcohol and drugs couldn't fix me. But surely good news and cake could.

I was wrong. I write a lot about how there is no messing

up, and I still believe this to be true. But there are golden moments of pivoting. Of tearing everything down to rebuild it.
And I have done this again and again.

I write this book not as an authority on finding your center. If
anything I'm about as off center as they come, and that is why I
qualify. I qualify for a seat in about every twelve-step program,
because I live every day in conversation with the Spirit of the
Universe about why I don't reach for distraction or someone
or something to fix me. Maybe this is what we are here for—to
look at what distracts us from our center. For me it's drugs, alcohol, coffee, sugar, and certainly the most mesmerizing high
of them all: love.

So I took eight months to live in Michigan, to host other
artists who were also diving deep, and to spend many nights
alone to see—what is it I am distracting myself from? And how
can I stay in the center? How can I stay in the mundane? How
can I continue this work in partnership or a new geographical
location?

What is maintenance like for me? What if I willingly and
gladly turned my life over to the care of a wondrous and caring
higher power—that I sometimes call god[1] and sometimes call
grass and never call myself?

---

1   A note on the word "God"/"god": I will use the word "god"/"God"/"goddess"
    throughout the book. It is genderless and lowercase and sometimes up-
    percase and it was whatever you want it to be. It is a higher power, the
    Spirit of the Universe, a blade of grass. I like having a god, because it's a
    quick short word that means "in the everything" to me, and by "every-
    thing," I mean something outside of myself. But I am part of the every-
    thing too. If you're triggered by the word "God, " that's okay too, but I'll
    keep using it and you can close your eyes and think of your own word.

What if I wasn't in charge? Or trying to fix everything? I am in charge of the work, of the inventory, of maintaining hope and admiration and generosity. But something much greater than myself is at the helm of this ship. Thank goddess, because this life is the *Titanic*, and like a true Gemini, I'm the couple holding hands going down with it.

In this book I promise to forgive myself, over and over again, as both an offering to you the reader, and to my intimate real-life community of family and friends. For in my suffering I am unavailable, unreachable, and unteachable.

As I write this, I feel my spine healing. After I received news that this book would indeed exist and I would be writing it, I shrank. I wanted to get so tiny and small and hide and never tell anyone I was going to write a book. And my spine collapsed beneath me. I don't mean this as a metaphor. A vertebra in my spine came out of place, I threw my neck out, and my lower back started hurting more than I'd known it could. What was my backbone telling me, the backspace, my support system? I was cowering from myself, so afraid of stepping into my own light.

That is my ego. Just like my ego can bring me to grandiose places, it can bring me into the *you are so undeserving* places. But this isn't about me. My fingertips fly over the keyboard as an act of devotion to the channeling process. These are words from another planet. A separate galaxy. My grandmothers are writing this; my dad's dead best friends are writing this (Bobby and Joe); Nan, who pulled me out of my mother's womb; my beloved former boss Marie Catrib is writing with me; my collaborator George is writing this from whatever heaven he catapulted to; Lucy, my childhood dog, is writing this.

We have a whole team of ancestors waiting for us to write with them. To share our words not because we have to or should, but because we are called to and we can.

Just before I wrote this, I wanted to reach for a vice. The moment we are ready to reach is the moment something truly divine is ready to come out of us. What if we didn't reach? What if we stayed in the center?

This is where we will go together. Not *if* we get knocked off, but when. And with the tools we learn for staying in the center longer.

You can do this. You can read this book. This book isn't here to fix you or heal you or make you better than everyone else. It's just to keep you in the middle lane for a little longer than you're used to and to help you get back faster. Or to love yourself when you're on the far left longer than you ever imagined you would be.

There is a great and unfettering love inside of me, that longs for joy and self-acceptance. I write this to cast a spell for myself and every reader—that we may devour joy and let it be a gift to those who could benefit.

CHAPTER 1

Practice

We start here, we begin with building our own practice. We will ride the wild waves together of many different feelings, situations, hopes, strategies, ways to give up, ways to give in, ways to get back. They are for you to add in and take out, just as you should with any practice. A practice is shape-shifting, transmutable, undefined, yet defined and rigid at the same time.

How can things be both/and? How can things be everything and nothing at the same time? This is what we are here to discover! My practice, across all mediums, is taking my own self-reflection and reporting it back to you in the form of books, zines, a weekly newsletter, my weekly radio show, dance videos and classes, and social media, and with my own voice right to your ears through online courses.

I wanted to begin our journey somewhere else. Somewhere deep, I wanted us to go straight to grief or to joy or to imposter syndrome. I wanted us to immediately dive into the work of noticing where finding ourselves and our identity in the world will save us on the individual and collective level. To tell you everything I know about vulnerability and rest and rejuvenation.

But that's part of getting to center. I always want to jump ahead. I want to skip every step, specifically the steps of my practice, to get to the end goal. There is no end goal, though. We never graduate. We are forever in the school of aliveness, and lesson 101 might seem trite, but I promise you this—it is not. It is exciting and it is plentiful, and it is yours. Your practice is yours.

It is my ultimate belief that everything is practice. In this beginning moment of exploring how we DO indeed get to our center—it is a budding and thriving practice that is my most consistent answer. We will soon jump to the fact that everything ends, so, brace yourself. Pace yourself, use this time to check in and dig deep—what IS my practice?

If you're already overwhelmed by the idea of committing to doing something every day, let me reassure you that is not my suggestion. While I have found huge transformation in having public and personal projects be done daily, I have also seen where this kind of commitment and my breaking of it have set me back. So let us begin with this: instead of calling the things we weave into our centering practice "daily rituals," let's just call them "THINGS TO RETURN TO." I.e.: morning pages, stretching, skateboarding, herbal infusions, Beach Monday, walking, hydrating, reading, quilting, dancing.

Because that's the thing! I believe we will always leave and we will always escape what we have set up for ourselves. I've set myself up for inner success just as many times as I've sabotaged it.

In setting up these "things to return to," we can start to sabotage ourselves less. Or maybe the exact same amount but we catch it earlier. We close the gap in time between self-sabotage and recognizing it. In this closing of the gap, we also form new ways of speaking to ourselves. If at this point you notice you are just a total asshole to yourself, that's okay. Defining your practice is a first step in healing an inner voice that is unkind. Focus on the simplicity of new pathways and new meanderings and ways to pivot to take you back to what works—each time with a little less *fuck you for leaving* and a little more *welcome back*.

I LOVE TO be around Ellen Rutt, a friend and collaborator and fellow Michigander. Ellen is an artist who never runs out of ideas and executes them with an urgency and specificity that always pushes me to do more, yet when I feel slow and unmotivated she is also a friend who reminds me of my inherent worthiness. In her studio one day in the fall of 2019, I spotted a photograph of myself from when we were at the ocean together where I lived in California in summer 2018. I borrowed a book of Michigan quilts from Ellen's library and was inspired to finish setting up my own studio at home. This experience reminded me how author and consultant Beth Pickens talks about how we need other artists—to visit their studios, to have them on our team, to open our eyes to what we didn't know we needed to see and remember. To remember our own practice by witnessing another's.

A few weeks before that visit to Ellen's studio, I had just

moved from one side of Michigan to the other. It felt like a bigger move than other moves—I had been running a residency from January to July of 2018, being single, traveling a lot. This move I found myself on the other side of the state, cohabitating with my partner, not hosting artists regularly/within a structure—and I found my level of work and work productivity had gone down.

I'd like to present to you a brief timeline of significant events before we dive into defining our practices. A lot has happened in the last decade that led me to being able to identify my practice, and constantly reorient myself to it, and it may be helpful for you as the reader to get it all at once.

Thursday, June 2, 1988: I am born while Mercury is retrograde in Grand Rapids, MI.

Spring 1993: I make a home movie dance video to "Rhythm Nation" by Janet Jackson.

1996–2006: Living the ballerina life.

May 2010: I get a BFA in dance from the University of Michigan.

May 17, 2011: I quit drinking! I also meet John.

May 25, 2013: I marry John!

July 2013: I open Have Company, an artist residency/podcast/shop/gallery in Grand Rapids.

Summer 2015: Personal Practice and *How to Not Always Be Working* the zine are born.

May 25, 2016: I get divorced from John.

October 2016: I close Have Company and move to California.

March 2018: I realize I am gay!

October 2018: *How to Not Always Be Working* the book
  is born.

January 2019–July 2019: I move back to Michigan and
  MOVE IN WITH JOHN to host an artist residency
  together.

February 2019: I meet Jackie.

September 2019: Jackie and I move to the other side of
  Michigan, into the woods.

March 2019: We move to New Mexico, where Jackie gets
  a new job as a Santa Fe Hotshot.

Of course, about one million other things happen in this timeline. I fall in love a ton, I get dumped, I move houses, I gain new friendships, I lose some too.

But what kept me with myself the whole time was my practice.

As you can see, and as you will learn—I begin a lot. We always have the ability to begin again, when something ends or goes wrong or doesn't go the way we expected it to. We can begin again.

ON BEGINNINGS

Beginnings, the most disorienting of them all. Almost everyone I work with is so afraid to begin, and once they do, the relief is so sweet. We all have the ability to explore what stops us from starting and examine why beginnings can be so disorienting (typically fear, past trauma, inability to focus, lack of clarity on the hope for the end result, too much attachment to the end result, assumptions around something being inadequate). Beginnings can sometimes be *too* exciting. Adrenaline hits the body, and we are distracted, the wildness of falling in love, the rush of starting something new. It comes back to obsession again—how can we begin perfectly? Am I cool enough? Someone else starts to validate how cool you are, so you forget to access your inner cool/power/work because you are getting the high from somewhere else. Whether it is small or big, beginning something can often be the hardest thing. I'll road map how to love yourself through a new beginning.

PRACTICE, NOT PERFECTION

The hardest part of starting really seems to be loving yourself through it. It's clunky—it's going to be so clunky—and that's okay. It's supposed to be; you have never done this before. Not in this exact way. Every new relationship, I REALLY think I get it. *I've done this before! I have loved before, been a good partner, called someone back—how can this be any different?* But with each new person we love—whether romantic or platonic—we are matching two lived experiences that have never been matched before. When you begin again, you also are tasked with the experience of leaning into not knowing. You don't know how it will go, and you might have to pull out the oldest tools in your toolbox.

LET IT BE A COMFORTABLE MYSTERY

IT IS SO DIFFERENT! IT IS A NEW MYSTERY—which we should be so grateful for. But every new thing is a new thing. The second I am writing this sentence is a new beginning from the last sentence. When you fall in love again, it's a new beginning. Yes, you get to integrate every single thing you learned from the last thing. But this new person, this new love, this new beginning—will be nothing like the last one. In a good way. Let it be good. Let yourself receive new lessons by having a new beginning. Try going slower. Maybe this time try going faster. Lean in a little more.

HOW TO CHANGE YOUR MIND

So, you've made a decision—you've told everyone that the decision has been made and you are ready for your new beginning. You feel excited and in control by having the agency to make said decision. After the decision is made, though, there may be times it could occur to you it is an incorrect decision.

Immediately would be one. You make the decision to tell someone out loud, and then you almost instantly know it is not correct. Or it could take a few weeks and the more you tell people, the more it's not in alignment.

So we ask ourselves: When we make a decision, is it better to tell everyone or to not tell anyone?

There are three options I come to when processing:

Processing alone

Processing with friends and others

Processing one-on-one with a mentor/therapist/
   sponsor/psychic, etc.

I find that a balance between all three can be most harmonious. If I do too much talking out loud all the time to friends
without checking in with myself or a professional, I can really
run myself thin. I can talk myself into anything, and I can talk
myself out of anything.

The important thing to remember is, you are allowed to
change your mind. Anytime, always. You are always freaking allowed to change your mind. In fact, I hope you do. The amount
of shame I attach to myself when I want to do something different is so strong, but the softer I am when I greet myself in
the shift, the more success I have getting back on the beam.

EXERCISE: WARMING INTO WORKING

When I teach dance class, I borrow something from my teachers called "warming into working," and I can't help but apply
this to every other beginning or practice. It's okay to warm
into the working, to the practice, to the beginning. There are
so many ways to approach a beginning—from repeating the
same task over and over again to slowing down after you've
gone really fast. Mirroring the person next to you, reversing a
movement. Again, these are in dance composition terms, but
they are applicable to all entry points.

What is your practice NOW? What do you want your practice to be? Let us dream up all the things that a practice is and

what a practice can do for us. This is sort of a DREAM STATE assuming great abundance. So even if you aren't fully there yet or believing it, I want you to begin the consideration process of what a practice would look like for you regardless of time, privilege, money, space, etc.

My vision for my own practice is in a constant state of flux, of rearranging. A hopeful eagerness, a sense of urgency, and also a playful curiosity is how I vision my own practice—often changing every day.

While I do believe in daily habits, I also believe in self-softness—a form of being soft with yourself when (not if) you break habits or promises to yourself. While the creation of rituals and practice is of the utmost importance, we also have to find ways to bring ourselves—you guessed it—back to our center. This is the idea we are here to explore together. That I will remind us of countless times. I am reminding myself, and I am reminding you.

I see this everywhere I turn: this overwhelming shame of getting lost, or not remembering. Our media intake is, honestly, unreal. It's not a small thing. It is a wild, wild thing. We are consuming more in a single day than people used to in a whole year. I won't necessarily ask you to stop doing this, to stop using social media, listening to the news, engaging with articles altogether. But I will provide tools for defining and building your practice—whether it's in art, business, activism, your personal life, your rituals, self-care, community care, or something else you'd like to vision.

Building a foundation filled with practice and visions will help you return to your center in faster and more efficient ways. Sometimes it will seem impossible to return. That's what this book is for. The constant return. The forever remembering.

We will forget. You will absolutely forget. If there is one thing I can promise you, it's that you will forget. To make art, to take care of yourself, your friends, your body, your mind. And it is in this forgetting that we must remember. To cultivate a practice of remembering is to return to your center.

So—what IS your practice? Maybe you're ready to birth a new project into the world, an online business, a client service, visions for your sacred morning rituals.

ART PRACTICE VISION
BUSINESS PRACTICE VISION
PERSONAL PRACTICE VISION
RITUAL PRACTICE VISION

I keep practice after each of these topics because I believe it keeps our work/life free of harsh end goals. If you want to make goals—amazing. Your practice will absolutely help you get to them. Someone asked me once (referring to my dance project Personal Practice), What are you practicing for? I felt stunned—*Hmmmm*, I thought. *What AM I practicing for?* I am just practicing. Sure, sometimes I teach, sometimes I perform. But those are also forms of my practice. I am practicing for the sake of practicing.

In all of the exercises throughout this book, I suggest taking markers and blank pieces of paper to write these things out. You could also use a document on your computer. I am a fan of using the marker-and-paper method and taping them to the wall.

From *Free Play: Improvisation in Life and Art* by Stephen Nachmanovitch: "The Western idea of practice is to acquire a skill. It is very much related to our work ethic, which enjoins us to endure struggle or boredom now in return for future rewards. The Eastern idea of practice, on the other hand, is to create the person, or rather to actualize or reveal the complete person who is already there. This is not practice for something, but complete practice, which suffices unto itself. In Zen training they speak of sweeping the floor, or eating, as practice. Walking as practice."

Keeping this in mind—make lists of what's included in your practice. You don't have to be poetic or write in full sentences. It can be fluid. Write words, lists, ideas that are part of your practice. Once we are clear on our practices, we can use them to transform ourselves and the world. We can use them to remember how to return to ourselves.

These exercises are to be done with a detachment to making or earning money. We can always be rearranging these parts of our practice. Sometimes my dance practice makes money; sometimes it does not. Of course, what is listed in "business practice" would hopefully be generating your income. But at this point in the process, let's enjoy a radical detachment from capitalism and how it exists within our practice.

There may be overlap in these categories. In part this draws from my last book, *How to Not Always Be Working*, breaking down what comes from where and how they are separate.

In my case, things from each of these categories can fall into my work, my work practice if you will. This is part of my life of sharing what I know and how I live. However, in the clarity of these lists, I can know that if my business practice is feeling off, my ritual practice might be the thing that brings me back to a more harmonious state.

ART PRACTICE VISION

Your art practice vision is anything that feeds your creative spirit. For instance, my sewing and quilting practice falls into this category. I don't make money off of the practice itself. Every now and again I will teach a quilting class, which generates income. Or I use my sewn pieces as backdrops for photos or promotions for my class. I do, however, stay detached from the "how" of how they'll be used.

In 2018, I got into painting small watercolors just for pleasure, and in 2019 I enjoyed painting skateboards for myself, residents, and friends. This has been another fun way to make art and be creative but not have it directly linked to income generation.

BUSINESS PRACTICE VISION

Your business practice vision is anything within your job, career, or business that you practice. As well as when and how often these practices do or could occur. Remember, these are visions. These can reach further than where they currently are.

If you have a job where you work for someone else, this could be a research practice. For instance, if you are working at an architecture firm, you might want to sit at the library for a while and research different building techniques that could inform your practice.

PERSONAL PRACTICE VISION

Your personal practice vision is what you do for you and only you. This does not mean you can never share it with the world. Or that it never makes money. But the initial impulse is to do something for yourself, with complete detachment to the outcome.

For me, this is dancing, recording the dance, and sharing it. Dancing is also a part of my art practice. Sometimes it is also part of my business practice. It is always a part of my research practice. But there are times when it is very important that it is personal. My personal growth is the first priority, and the benefits of sharing this practice are secondary.

Another form of personal practice would be REALLY sharing it with no one. Stretching in the living room, walking with headphones in, walking with no headphones in, swimming as far as you can go and never telling anyone you did it.

RITUAL PRACTICE VISION

Building rituals into our lives is a great and tangible way to bring ourselves back to center. Using flower essences, prayers, pulling cards from an oracle or tarot deck, building an altar, being in community with others in a sharing or support circle. A ritual could be infused into cooking for friends, making a gratitude list every night before you go to bed, journaling every morning—doing the same thing one day a week at the same time.

When I ran Have Company, we started a tradition called Beach Monday. It became the ritual that everyone who worked there, along with the visiting artist, would travel to the beach every single Monday. Rain, snow, sleet, hail, busy schedules, hard deadlines: we went to the beach.

It opened me up to how Lake Michigan is an ocean of possibility, no matter what the temperature. It's seen as a tourist vacation destination, covered in lakeside homes of the affluent, but we could always go there and walk down a free public trail to see what had emerged seasonally, to engage in the landscape in new ways.

An ever-changing Lake Michigan became my favorite thing. To sit on a frozen wave and look out into the horizon brought on a new awareness that can only come from building in consistent ritual. It also became a joy to share it with others.

o   o   o

REMEMBERING PRACTICE

Now that you've envisioned some of these categories, you might be afraid you will forget about them. I certainly forget and need reminders—often. Here is a list of more ethereal reminders to bring you back to your more concrete lists.

- Taking a bath in silence
- Lying on the ground (blanket or no blanket, your choice) and staring at the sky
- Chopping vegetables
- Going for a walk
- Stretching
- Throwing socks at the wall
- Chopping wood

While some of these are daily tasks required for survival or may seem mundane depending on your current situation, these are examples of things that bring me back into awareness and states of clarity. I don't try to categorize them or make them better or worse or more valuable than other things—they just are.

Make a list of what you always want to remember, and then refer to the remembering practices above to move toward them:

- I have a body, and I love this body.
- Eating snacks while I write or work helps me not reach for the phone or other distractions.
- I love seltzer.
- Baths help my back hurt less.
- The universe has an ultimate timeline, and I accept it.
- I have the tools I need to ask for help.
- Twelve-step meetings help me realign my thinking.

You can write these on a piece of paper and stick them on the wall, make a note on your phone, share them with a friend—whatever will help you stay accountable to the practice of remembering.

o o o

Part of my Saturn return lessons were to let things stir for less time. Every 29.5 years (roughly), Saturn returns to the exact place that it was when you were born. This often shakes up people's lives, revealing new truths and life plans. For instance, mine sort of looked cliché—gets divorced, moves across country, comes out. There are the more "factual" things that happen as well as the internal lessons that coincide. I was able to see how quickly I can start to address a problem, a habit, a feeling, rather than let it sit inside of me for "too long."

I say "too long" because I've been reflecting on how my defects of character aren't always removed as quickly as I want because they are sometimes still serving me. I get frustrated to experience the same loop over and over again. But I feel myself get faster every time. At noticing it, naming it, moving through it.

Part of our practice should be to be around art, especially if you are an artist. Part of our practice should be to be with other people who think like we do. Not in the insular bubble way where people pat you on the back for thinking the same thoughts as them in a self-congratulatory way. I mean people who see us. People who see our pain and understand it. People who want the same kind of world as we do.

At the same time, it can also be a part of our practice to see the differences in other people. And sometimes these are the same people. My partner, artist and wildland firefighter Jackie Barry, made a flag for an art show that said "LESS CURATION / MORE CONVERSATION"—a great reminder to us all that we curate all of our spaces. Our social media feeds, our dinner parties and gatherings—what we consume is closely curated.

Sometimes this is for safety, but sometimes I find it to be pleasing to get out of my comfort zone and practice being around new voices—often ones that clash with my own. And then, when I see through to our similarities, it creates a closeness and a communal transformation.

Being understood and seeking to understand is my newest practice. To love unconditionally. Which doesn't mean to love someone or something without seeing any of their flaws or having hard conversations about what could be better. But it means NO CONDITIONS. That my love is not based on if the dishes are done, the bills are paid on time, the clothes are put away; that I am getting exactly what I want when I want it. It is a practice of seeing the good, and we live in a world where it is so easy to want to pick out the bad apples. One small bruise, and we kick it to the curb; we don't even check to see if it's worth a bite.

This usually happens to me when I go through transitions or shifts, which if I'm radically honest with myself is: usually, always, often. It normally takes me getting to sort of a bottom to climb out. I am always trying to shorten the bottoming-out-during-transitions gap, but I think I am also activated by the climbing out.

This leads us back to less shame around our practice, because climbing out is itself a practice. Sometimes we scramble to the top; sometimes we fall halfway up the climb and have to start over. As much as I am dedicated to not measuring our worth by our productivity, when I am not meeting easy standards in my work, I know something is off. Generally, this signal comes in the sign of a physical pain or glitch in the matrix of my body.

You may notice how much content many creators and artists share on social media, making really beautiful, shareable memes and quotes and free things on their website, etc. The comparison trap can make me feel so small and lazy. Or that my life must be boring if I don't have anything to showcase to the world today. This is why I broke up our categories for us, that we may be blessed with many different kinds of practices. As soon as I start to practice comparison, I separate myself from the universal truth that I am right on time.

First of all, my standards are always so much higher than they need to be in terms of outside presentation. Some seasons I make "less content." In quotations because these are standards I have invented out of thin air. But during those seasons I am usually finding myself in more ways than I knew I could. And this is tiring behind-the-scenes work! Plus, not every small business/artist/human is going to look the same or be able to do the same.

If I am "doing less" than other people, that is okay. How many times did I look like I was doing so much, producing so much work, and yet I was in a horrible relationship and hating my life? I poured everything into outside forces and projects instead of myself.

This is part of harmonizing our practices. It isn't about finding the perfect balance. In the last few years, my private and personal life has needed a lot more tending to than my public life. Or, it needed the same amount it always needed—I just actually listened! My listening practice was heightened.

o   o   o

WHEN YOU WAKE UP, ASK YOURSELF: WHAT IS THE MOST LIFE-GIVING THING I CAN DO FOR MYSELF RIGHT NOW? That might not look the same every day! But this question gives us pause—if "grab the phone and get the updates" fuels you—DO THAT FIRST! If it's going for a walk, kissing, playing with your kid or pet, reading—DO THAT. Let it be different each day. But let it be the sweet start that sets the tone for how you SEE THE WORLD TODAY! And remember—YOU CAN START YOUR DAY OVER AT ANY TIME!

Practice, over and over, practice.
Not just the practice of doing but the practice of
    remembering.
Which is also the process of becoming.

As I uncover, almost every day, some stone left unturned, I am grateful for the foresight to turn them over faster and to see what's under there. When I hide from myself, I hide from the world, and the more I practice not hiding, the more I see whatever has been stirring is just a gentle truth I already partly knew. And the whole truth is never as unmanageable as it was to hide from it.

o o o

Prayer For Practice

May my practice be easeful
May my practice be fruitful
May my practice be consistent
May my practice be easy to return
to when I am inconsistent
May my practice be fluid
May my practice be rooted in the unknown
May my practice be what I can return to
when I am far away from myself

CHAPTER 2

Commitment

When we look at practice, we look at commitment. What is it that we are committing to? What is the point of commitment? And when is it okay to break a commitment?

A lot of what I have been thinking about, writing about, and am presenting to you is about breaking commitments. How to do so with ease and grace, how to do so while still being in love with yourself and the world around you.

But I also believe in commitments. I see how they work for us, how they strengthen us, and how we can honor them for what they are or what they were, even if they shift. Sometimes I think, *What the hell is the point of even making a commitment if it seems we just live in a world of broken ones?* Well, faith, trust, hope, these we will address later, but I promise they are a part of the right now—a part of how we shape commitments in our own hearts and with others.

On New Year's Eve 2019, I did a handfasting ceremony with Jackie, to stay committed to her for the next 365 days. Not for forever, and not for one day at a time. Usually, I like to pick one of those two extremes. I am yours for an hour or I am yours for eternity, but God forbid I would be yours for a whole year. We set out to look at our visions for the future and the right now. How did we want it to feel, how did we want it to look, and how did we want our partnership to reflect our individual strengths?

I love this commitment because now we have a framework, something to strive for. Something to work at and work toward. With a longer time frame, we get to apply the one-day-at-a-time model. How can I, just for today, make sure to take time for myself—focus on my art practice, be outside—in service to myself and our partnership, so that our commitment may stay strong for this year and that many years of that practice could indeed lead to an even longer commitment of love?

So yes, I believe in commitments. Before you call me a non-believer or think everything I say is contradictory—I DO believe in commitments! I also believe in not hating ourselves if they don't go as planned.

But I think STRIVING for something is really cool, and something I forget to do sometimes. I believe that's why our simple but thorough handfasting ceremony felt so good. It wasn't lavish, it wasn't in front of a hundred people, I didn't share that we did it on social media or in my newsletter. But it feels really serious to me, to strive to stay true to Jackie for all of 2020.

To stay true to Jackie means to stay true to myself. To be a mirror to each other. Because we will want to quit. I wanted to quit a few days ago. I mean, not actually, but a part of me thought, *Can I really do this?*—so I took an alone retreat. Alone retreats are excellent ways to keep your commitments to other people, because they are really all about keeping the commitment to yourself.

I spent the first six months of 2018 ALONE. Every night alone in my bed, super stoked to be alone all the damn time. I lived in a huge house where I could always find a place to be very alone.

Cue to the second half of the year and into 2020: I live with my very hot and smart girlfriend and our very perfect dog in a beautiful town in New Mexico. However, when I don't have enough alone time, everyone starts to look like demons to me and I am the ice queen on my fire throne ready to melt and drown us all. Everything hurts me. My sensitivity levels are through the roof. Nothing can satisfy me. Nothing brings me joy. And I sure as hell don't like myself. So I go on an alone retreat.

And I would love to present to you my own visions to support you in YOUR own alone retreat. Commitment to self as a radical practice for survival.

o o o

How to Go Be the Fuck Alone

o Find a place you can sleep alone for the night. Maybe it's a friend's house who is out of town—maybe you spend forty-six dollars on one of those cute modern Motel 6 rooms—whatever you do, just FIND A PLACE YOU CAN REALLY BE ALONE; it could be a spare bedroom or even the couch.

- Remember that if you hate yourself and everyone around you it's going to be really hard to change the world even in small, tiny ways (you don't have to SAVE the world, but you do have to be nice).
- Bring your favorite books and your favorite snacks.
- Take a bath and do nothing else at the same time.
- Sleep in.
- Take breaks if you bring work, consider taking a solo dance party break.
- Make a list of actionable steps for social and Earth change—if you have the privilege of this alone space, use it to carve out new futures.
- Notice the signs that it's time for an alone retreat, like when your partner suggests you watch the new episode of *The L Word* separately and you take it as a personal attack and want to kill her. That would be a cue it is time to drive away and be alone with your thoughts.
- You can also just add more spaciousness into your day-to-day: have a coffee shop date alone, go on a walk, take a drive, go to the movies alone, etc.

SO, WHEN WE ask ourselves, *Is it really possible to keep commitments to others?* I think it's best to start with vague questions: *Are we committed to ourselves? And what exactly does that look like? And how do we dull the blow of breaking commitments?*

Maybe we begin by striking the word "break" from our talk

of commitment. We rearrange commitments; we shift them. We form new commitments, new devotions, new dedications.

I'd like us to look at two different ways "commitment" is defined:

A. The state or quality of being dedicated to a cause
B. An engagement or obligation that restricts freedom of action

Well, who wants that? Who wants restriction? Maybe some of you do, or maybe you're squirming thinking about a single thing restricting you. This is why people are so often "afraid of commitment"—or afraid of being restricted.

But what if our commitments were exactly in line with what we needed to feel complete freedom, complete autonomy within the structures of agreements that we make with ourselves and others?

Some of the most traditional and obvious things we think of when we think of commitment are "job" and "partnership." My life has been an ever-shifting renegotiation of both of these things, and the high level of self-forgiveness that comes with them.

We're told that keeping commitments means we are steadfast, we are trustworthy, we are worth something. This just isn't true. There has to be more spaciousness for us to breathe. There has to be more room for the commitment to not be true.

When I think of commitment and the benefits of its ever-shifting nature, I think of the book *Love Warrior* by Glennon Doyle. Glennon writes that her husband had been cheating on her since the beginning of their marriage. She managed to stay sober through this world-shattering news. They decided to stay together through deep work and personal discovery, and voilà, the book comes out: *Love Warrior*.

Shortly after, they ended their marriage, and Glennon coupled up with the greatest soccer player of all time, Abby Wambach. She and her husband remain dear friends and coparents, and the journey continues. She married Abby, they change the world separately and together, and we are bearing great witness. To me this was the ultimate example of publicly revealing one thing, in a literal *NYT* bestselling book, and then being like: *Actually, we have a new truth to present, a new commitment to consider.*

Where is the center in all of this? Only you can know. Someone could come to you with something they have been hiding forever. And maybe that new knowledge feels like it will certainly end the whole entire world. But really, it just opens up a new world for you. A new commitment to self.

That is the most important commitment. That is the only commitment that really matters. Because at any moment, you could be holding tightly, and someone else could decide they are no longer committed in the same way you are.

The *Boston Globe* interviewed me for their podcast *Love Letters*—the topic of the season being "How do you know?" How did I know when to end my marriage? How do you know when to GET married? How do you know when your commitment to yourself and to the energetic structure matches? What if it stops matching?

This whole book is an attempt to uncover what is hiding beneath for fewer surprises, while at the same time honoring that every single day is a surprise, every single day has a newness that we can't know until we're in it.

With my online students we look at making daily and weekly goals, keeping them, and not being total monsters to ourselves when we don't keep these goals. THESE COMMITMENTS.

Staying committed to self and to others can feel restricting, as I mentioned before. It can feel like freedom is being taken away from us. I mean, it's curious to me how many monogamous folks cheat on each other, and how many open/poly/monogamish folks I know don't even sleep with other folks most of the time. The commitment to monogamy suffocates some while for others it might create the perfect container. I have found that a more open model of partnership allows me to feel like my choices can shift when I need them to.

What stays the same, though? My deep and unwavering commitment to self. My deep and unwavering commitment to my partner. If this shifts, it will not be because we broke a rule, but because the commitment needs to look different.

In asking, "How do you know?" I think there are a series of questions we can look to. How do we know when it's time to shift the commitment? A change in commitment doesn't necessarily mean an ending. It could mean an ending to a chapter, but it doesn't have to mean bailing altogether on what you said you would do.

AH! What we said we would do! The shame, the utter despair! At having to tell people. Quietly, loudly, writing a damn memoir about it. How many commitments have we stayed in so long simply because the pain of TELLING people was too much? Not even just the pain itself of removing ourselves from the situation, but the pain of being public about it. About how it alters our identity.

o   o   o

Okay, so—How. Do. We. Know? When it's time to "break" the commitment. Time to make a new commitment.

How does my body feel when I am around this person?
Can I breathe deeply?
Am I my complete self?
Does this relationship help me find who my complete
    self is?
Am I able to take care of myself when I'm with them?

If the answers to these questions shock you or are different than maybe you thought—don't panic!

Our centers are strong. Even when they are weak and feel broken and murky and unclear. They exist within us to carry this information into the unknown that is ahead. You have the tools. We will continue to build them as we go along together.

Seeing things clearly is scary as hell. Just unequivocally terrifying. It took me thirty-one years to start regular therapy, after over eight years of sobriety and plenty of trauma and mental health issues. Because seeing the whole thing felt too big, felt like too much.

And that was my cue. My fear around my commitment to my new partnership ending and realizing: Am I even committed to myself?

I don't buy into the whole idea of "you have to love yourself completely before you can love someone else." That bullshit would keep most of us all sorts of lonely and fucked up and alone forever, I'm pretty sure. Because figuring out how to love yourself takes a lot longer than ages thirteen to twenty-one, aka when you start realizing maybe you hate yourself and should figure out how not to so you can date someone.

So, loving myself completely. Right now, yes, doing great. Two hours ago, really low, just, like, totally depraved and certain I would never be anything in this one precious life. But two hours later, we're doing great! Why? SELF-COMMITMENT.

I made some food. I sat down to write. I stayed committed. And that's what I saw. I might not be able to love anyone fully if I don't stay committed to figuring out how to love myself. There is no graduation ceremony for this work. There is no diploma. I don't get a piece of paper that says *YOU DID IT—you finally figured out how to not let your inner voice beat you to a pulp right before you sit down to work.*

The center is where we must go! We must climb through the dark leaves of nothingness. The confusion, the chaos, and the unimaginable pain.

ACCOUNTABILITY

Now that we've given ourselves big permission to NOT stay committed, let's talk about the joy and power of keeping them. And how the hell to even keep them.

When I started my dance documentation project, Personal Practice, on Instagram, I wanted a place to put my dancing because I had lost my commitment to this practice. It wasn't consistent; I wasn't performing or teaching. In 2010, I graduated with a BFA in dance. Between 2010 and 2015, I danced here and there, performing sometimes, studying with my mentors, but it was sparse, and it wasn't enough for me.

I found that the key to the success of my one-plus-year commitment to dancing every day was accountability. I told the world I was going to dance every day. I had a place to put it. And I only had to do it for fifteen seconds. I could do it for longer; I often did. I was able to stay detached from how it felt for others. I wasn't committed to the followers, the witnesses. I was only committed to myself, but I knew they were there. Viewers gathering inspiration or thinking I was dumb. Making fun of me or changing their own lives by dancing in their own living rooms. It was everything, and it was nothing. That's the thing about commitment, the other side doesn't have to be equal. And there will be waves of participation.

Whether it is a personal commitment in love or career, or a commitment to self that you make in front of a few thousand people—it's a classic case of taking care of your side of the street. By setting up this system of accountability for myself, I was able to keep the promise to myself to dance every day for a year. After about a year and a half, I felt like my task was complete. I'd gotten what I needed. I felt like a dancer again. I always was, but I SAW myself again. I started performing again, teaching, practicing, making longer work, collaborating.

This opened me up to a knowing of myself I hadn't had before. For the next three years, I would continue to make dance videos and share them, self-publishing a book about it, teaching intensives, making music videos, and connecting to my commitment to self along the way. I announced the shift publicly, but I kept my own parameters to myself. I know it's there if I need it. If I feel myself wishing for more dancing, for more movement—I know I can record myself and have a place to share it. And because I never expected anything from those witnessing, I was able to change the commitment whenever I wanted to.

o   o   o

TINY GOALS

Tiny goals in commitment making can ease our minds. In my sobriety, I often refer to the one day at a time model, and also celebrate that I only have to do anything one day at a time. Some days feel like an eternity, though, and we explore the next-right-thing model: What in god's world can I accomplish in the next ten minutes? And then when that ten minutes is up, I will make a new goal.

I've been making pivot lists and quick lists. What can I be committed to in this moment of total and complete chaos?

Example Pivot List:

- Phone a friend
- Read an article
- Go on a walk
- Donate money—financial generosity
- Make a quick list

Quick List:

- Pee
- Eat snack
- Pay phone bill
- Email Kate
- Send form

These pivot moments help me when my commitment to self-starts to feel threatened. When I am totally off track, on the outskirts of center but close enough that I can grab a pen and paper. pivot lists also feel like a reminder to WHAT I am committed to outside of myself in the first place.

WHAT AM I COMMITTED TO

Being an excellent friend
Being an excellent partner
Being informed about the state of affairs in my
    community and in the world
Wealth redistribution—giving money to queer
    organizations that are in line with my own visions for
    my life and community; giving money to residencies,
    therapy funds, Patreons of BIPOC, who are creating
    the kind of new futures I want to see in the world
Antiracism and social justice education and research
Being generous
The earth and being outside
Writing and sharing my story

CONSIDERATIONS ON HOW TO GIVE

You might be overwhelmed! There are so many mutual aid funds, GoFundMes, fundraisers, and nonprofits that need our help.

Here Are Some Examples of My Personal Process—They Are Built Off of the Main Question, "What Do I Have Access to in the World/What Future Do I Want to See?"

- Grand Rapids, MI, made me the person I am today > I want the people in that place to thrive, so I did a fundraiser for the Grand Rapids Mutual Aid Fund
- I receive weekly therapy > I want to lift up the mental health of Black women, so I make a monthly donation to The Loveland Foundation
- I didn't feel I had the resources I needed as a queer youth > I make occasional donations to the Grand Rapids Pride Center
- I love providing a free weekly newsletter and I believe in supporting queer brown femme writers with $$$ > So I pay the monthly subscription for Fariha Róisín's newsletter
- I am an author who believes in independent bookstores > I want them to exist post Covid, so I donate to their GoFundMes
- I live on occupied land and am also a newcomer to New Mexico > I donate to the Navajo Nation
- I am an artist and I love art > I buy or donate to queer/trans/BIPOC artists now and always

The amount you donate completely depends on your financial reality—which for many of us is CONSTANTLY CHANGING. I use a mix of light budgeting and intuition when deciding what to donate. I'll often send things in threes, like $33 to an individual's Venmo or $333 to an organization because that feels magical to me. You can send one dollar and share it in your stories even if you have 15 followers. There are many ways to lift up voices, but I do believe the smallest actions and donations add up.

I didn't make this up—and I also didn't wait to feel financially comfortable to start! I learned how to do this from a lot of different friends, teachers, etc., who taught me how to show up as a person with privilege. Doing it this way keeps me out of white saviorism or guilt—keeping the focus on "what kind of world do I want to see" keeps me in a space of hope and turns my privilege into action

WHEN THESE COMMITMENTS start to go by the wayside, that is my cue that I am off center. As I mentioned before, this is what brought me to therapy: this feeling that the only things that were keeping me "in" my center were my partnership and my addictions. Things that made me feel safe but weren't actually fulfilling my destiny.

In the past, I would get rid of them. Just quit the addiction, quit the relationship. Run as fast as I could, and all I would do is replace it with something else. New person, same spirals. Not this time—this time I get to look at what is beautiful and good.

Jackie works as a wildland firefighter for about half the year.

So we go through two very different seasons of togetherness—one that includes a lot more time apart and more spaciousness. Our seasons of togetherness are also met with a lot of spaciousness that we do our best to insert in the day-to-day. But when I forget what I am committed to, my fears arise in new ways. No matter how often we are together or apart, it's important to me to apply the same principles of my commitment to self/art/work.

When I make my list of commitments, short as it is, I also see how expansive they are. And when we both stay committed to ourselves, our commitments to each other will bloom and blossom and be everlasting. Everlasting doesn't mean it will always look the same. In fact, it brings me great joy to know that it will stay mysterious. That the commitment might change. That's the thing about these forests Jackie maintains—they burn to the ground in order to regrow. To constantly change—to become new again. And in her fearlessness and dedication and commitment to the trees and the Earth, I am reminded to look within to see where my commitment needs fine-tuning.

When you make your own list of commitments, know that they can change. Know that they *will* change.

The biggest commitment I ever made was to marry John. I was twenty-three when I made that decision. The commitment shifted within the container of marriage. To open it up and to see other people: this fed us and made us stronger. At some point within the commitment change, though, I lost myself. I lost my center. John maintained his, which lead us to mutually deciding our marriage was no longer sustainable.

Our vows never included being together forever; they included staying true to ourselves and loving each other and always being family. Those are commitments we've kept.

From the time of our divorce in 2016 to the end of 2018, we communicated lightly. We stayed loving and kind, we went through a few communication bumps, and we returned over and over to our commitment—to be loving and kind and be listeners to each other's experiences.

In the winter of 2019, we took a big leap. We decided to move into a house together in Grand Rapids, MI, and run an artist residency together for seven months. Yes, two divorced people decided to live under the same roof and work together and make magic together and learn together and grow together.

It was weird at first. The first ten days in the house, it was just the two of us. John had been there for a few months already, his things settled into their places. I opened up the cabinet and there was my favorite bowl, which I hadn't seen in three years—a ceramic masterpiece I had gifted him for his twenty-ninth birthday. Now, a thirty-three-year-old John stood in front of me, ready to go on this wild ride with me. Fears intact, hope instilled—a basket I bought at a thrift store in 2012 filled with his wool blankets. Our objects were in the same place. Paintings he'd given me for Christmas, things we'd bought together, things we'd taken, things that used to be ours and were ours again.

I was worried I would feel sad. I was worried it would remind me of how we had failed. A narrative I thought I had released myself from reemerged. I was worried I would wonder, *What if we had fixed this?*

Those feelings never showed up. Which also reminds me how much time we spend worrying how something we'll feel when we don't ever end up experiencing it.

It took us about a month to settle into our new commitment. We spent those first few weeks feeling more like coworkers and collaborators, trying to understand how we fit together in this new form.

John left for six weeks to work on a project in Guatemala while I stayed home facilitating the residency and also traveling on the West Coast. During this time, Jackie came into my life, John went through emotional tests that led him to reaching out to me, and when he returned, something clicked into place. This person is my forever family; my love for him is everlasting. Our new commitment was so much better than the old one we made.

During this time, I was working on the commitment to be single, and John was dating someone and trying to figure out if he could stay committed to someone else who desired a deeper commitment. We witnessed each other finding ourselves each day—as partners. We were new partners, partners in cocreation and staying alive and eating food together. Partners in navigating the world and how it works.

Find what you are committed to. By doing so, you clear the path for the return to center. We will carve this path together because it is the way in and it is the way out. And when nothing seems to be working, make a new list—"What I am committed to today?" may be very different from "what I am committed to tomorrow?"

○   ○   ○

Diligent Prayer for Better Phone Boundaries and Commitment to Self

Good spirit
May you guide us in better phone boundaries
May our commitment to ourselves be rooted
in looking away from the bright light of the
screen and into the bright light of ourselves
May we put the phone down when we want to
May we pick it back up when we are ready
Good spirit please take away my worry of FOMO
Please help me see that the right now in front of
me is all the magic I have ever dreamt of, and
if it is not lead me back to my commitments
and my practice to better do thy will, thy will
of looking away from the god damn phone

○   ○   ○

WHETHER IT'S FROM the part about phones in *How to Not Always Be Working* or my zine about the pains of social media, it is no mystery that I am a garden-variety phone addict. I have tried so many different things, and it can be so sad to not be able to control it, even when you try to put limits on yourself.

So I wanted to share an experience I had working on this phenomenon of mind, body, and spirit that has me trapped.

I suffer from a spine pain that is generally a psychosomatic result of holding on to emotions, feelings, trauma, etc. I generally work with craniosacral practitioners to alleviate this pain and get to the source. At one of my visits with Rachel Knapp, who has been my go-to for hands-on healing for almost seven years, new information emerged.

What came up about my current addiction spirals was this lack of benevolent divination. All the places in my spine and mind where I was blocking god became clear. I hadn't been praying or tapping into source, and was overly strung out from the screen.

I also had a vision of my grandmother Marlys, a quilter herself, handing me this cream piece of fabric cut into the shape of a rainbow to put on my altar to encourage digital minimalism.

SO, I went home. I built an altar, cut out the cream piece of fabric, and felt connected to my ancestors, and the Earth! I ended up turning my phone off promptly at 10 P.M. and have done so many days since and don't turn it on until my morning pages, daily readings, and card pulls are finished. Around the same time, I quit coffee and started drinking dandy blend (a noncaffeinated mixture made up of dandelion and chicory root). I started reading at night. I started stretching more. Drinking a ton of water every day.

My phone addiction got bad again when I started using an app to fall asleep, and then voilà—I was bringing the phone into bed and staring into its void late into the night (of course I needed an app to knock me out then!) and then first thing in the A.M. scrolling for at least an hour.

I guess what I am saying is god, alarm clocks, body work, your ancestors, and divination are the answer to your phone prayers. Even when we KNOW our willpower could help us with our limits, I truly believe that turning toward a limitless higher power is what can really save us. Feet in dirt work well too. I love you! You're not alone!

o   o   o

PRAYER FOR COMMITMENT

May your commitments be strong
May your commitments to yourself be boundless
May your commitment to self always come
first, because without that there is nothing
May your broken commitments be
cherished as good tries
May these good tries be their own divine chapters of life
May you be a spectacle of light amongst the chaos
May you strive for better commitment
and bigger ones every year
May they change with the seasons
And may you change with them

CHAPTER 3

Everything Ends

Everything ends. It's a fact. It's a promise. You will always forget, and everything will end. These truths do not have to be scary, and they do not have to derail you. In fact, I hope knowing them will bring you great relief and rest in GETTING to know them, that with this acceptance will come an ultimate form of growth and blooming.

There are two kinds of endings: ones we choose and the ones we do not. They can be equally painful, and yet they also have their own very distinct pain. Endings are a common offender for knocking us off our center. A partnership ends, a life ends, a job ends, everything is in upheaval. Our list of rememberings becomes obsolete. What's the point of staying true, staying on the path, when even an attempt at finding our center seems impossible?

Even with the sweet relief of natural freedom that comes with some endings, things will still be different. A truth of being alive, though, is that things are always different. We end our meal. We end a phone call. We end an email. Things are ending all around us, and we move through it with ease.

Acceptance of endings is the first step in seeing the sunset in the everything. Every day the sun sets. Every single day. What would it look like to see an ending as a sunset? Unless you're in Alaska during the summer solstice.

My marriage ending was one of my biggest endings. Lots of relationships end—and some marriages last for two months. Many marriages are much shorter than unmarried partnerships that last twenty years and then end. The word "divorce" carries such a big and unnecessary weight. Sometimes in conversation I just say "when I ended a five-year partnership" rather than "when I got divorced."

But there is something specific about marriage that comes with its painful ending. While I mentioned before that my vows never stated that I would always be married—I did proclaim that I would take great care of our partnership in front of a few hundred people, signed some legal documents, and had at least some vision that I would stay married to John.

So when this wasn't true, my great fear was how I would tell people that we'd "broken" our commitment. So much of my fear in the ending was about breaking a commitment and public approval or disapproval.

Here's the thing about endings—people are going to have their feelings about them. Big feelings that we do not get to control or advise them on or make better for them. We can't control how other people feel about our endings.

In turn, if you have feelings about someone else's ending, instead of projecting all your fears and worries onto them, consider looking inward to see what is coming up for you. Is it causing you grief to remember what it was like when you ended something?

Ending can also feel really good. When you end something that isn't serving you anymore, the newness can pour in. You know the old saying: "When one door closes, another one opens." I have found that closing one door builds entire new realities. Whole houses of rebirth and renewal grow in the shade of the door that closed.

The second-hardest thing I ever ended was Have Company. It was a place of my dreams, a clubhouse for everything and everyone that I loved. It started as a zine that I made at Shared Space Studio in Pentwater, MI, in 2012. I had become obsessed with Woody Guthrie's "New Years Rulin's."

Some of my favorites he wrote in this epic list: Take Bath, Listen to Radio a lot, Keep Hoping Machine Running, Have Company but Don't Waste Time, Dance Better, Love Everybody.

"Have company, but don't waste time" became a guiding light for me. I had been sober for a little over a year, and all I could think about was how much time I had wasted being blackout drunk and on drugs. I wanted a new life, and I wanted this new way of being alive to stick. I realized that having company, being with others, was my favorite way to not waste time. I was always engaged and excited when I was around my friends. This would prove to keep me not just occupied, but alive.

So after Have Company existed as a tiny zine, I took a trip to Portland where a shop in a camper is on every corner. I thought—*THIS IS IT! I could make my own tiny zine shop in a camper and fill it with art and all the things I love.* So in the fall of 2012, that is what I did, and Have Company became a little shop in a camper. It was a hit! The people loved it, and paying my friends for their work felt amazing. When winter hit and the snow fell on the camper, it became clear that many months out of the year would not permit this special endeavor to continue.

In July of 2013, after I got married, I opened up shop at 136 South Division. Have Company started as simply a shop, and over the next three years it grew into an artist residency, a podcast, a gallery, a classroom space, a space for people to pop in and share their art and their hopes and their pain with one another.

It's my favorite place I've ever been. It was a sunbeam in the winter and a shadow mirror in the bright summer light. It was a place that came from everything I couldn't find, and then it taught me everything I didn't know I needed to know.

After I got divorced, I moved into the back of the shop, into the space that I had been using to host residents. It was the first time I'd ever lived alone. It was scary and it was sweet, and then, like lightning, I was struck with the readiness to leave.

I didn't want to keep open hours anymore. Have Company had begun to grow into its own experiment of a public space, to take on its own energy, while my own public presence was growing. I was both detached from Have Company as a business and also one with it. In some ways, I couldn't see how we were separate, and this caused confusion within me and others.

I don't think it's bad to feel like you ARE your business, but I also see the importance of knowing you are not your business.

We are our work, and we are not our work. There is this gray area that sometimes serves us and then other times can make us lose ourselves in it all.

I decided I would move to California. I would close Have Company. It would end. In the moment of this decision, I was so ready to leave I couldn't see the grief that would later come. I think quick decisions sometimes protect us from the pain that is to follow. I choose to say "protect" rather than "mask" because I don't always think we're ready to see how much something is going to hurt. If we were, we might not allow the ending to occur.

Sometimes I joke that in order to separate myself from Have Company and return to myself, my center, I could have just taken a walk around the damn block. But in my true tornado form, I thought it best to sell every object I owned and pack up my Subaru and drive about as far away as I could. Both are right. Both could have worked. This whole life is just a series of choosing to either walk around the block or go out as far as we can. And over and over we gain new information about what works and what doesn't.

If you're ready to end something but feel numb, know there is nothing wrong with you. Or, if it feels incessantly sad, that also doesn't mean it's correct to stay IN it.

o o o

So—how do we KNOW when it's time to end something?

One thing that I have found through my own research of ending things left and right is that sometimes you actually don't know. You could go to twenty therapists and do your morning pages for years and meditate for two hours a day and make a few Venn diagrams and ask your psychic and pull a tarot card from all twenty decks you bought impulsively—and still, the answer to end or not end is nowhere in sight. I will say that morning pages tend to get me as close to my truth as anything else. Morning pages are an exercise presented by Julia Cameron in her book *The Artist's Way*—three pages of free writing to be done first thing upon waking. I find that when I do them—my practice or re-centering as dialogue AND transformation is in better alignment with the universe.

It's a pull-off-the-Band-Aid, close-your-eyes-and-jump-off-the-cliff moment. And you get to know the sweet relief that everything ends, but you know what doesn't have to end? Your commitment to yourself. Your dedication to yourself. **To your own process of becoming. You are becoming! With every ending you are becoming more of yourself.**

When I moved to California, I kept the idea of Have Company alive. I kept calling my podcast Have Company for another year, interviewing artists and humans that excited and inspired me. I was finishing my book about Personal Practice, and something came over me—Have Company had been a place; it wasn't just an idea. It started as an idea, it became a thriving business, it became a physical place, and the podcast was a way to document the residents.

Places and people are mourned differently. While a lot of content and ideas and experiences were birthed out of Have Company, it was also a physical space. A container for very real and transformative experiences. A place that became my home when I moved out of my house with John. A place that saw a lot of crying and dance parties and learning experiences.

Places and people can also be mourned the same way. There is, in some ways, less of a catastrophe of the heart when it's a place that we leave, or that leaves us. But we still attach memories and scents and interactions that we no longer have in that specific place. It's allowed to hurt just as bad.

Once I had been gone for about a year, I felt like Have Company was . . . no longer mine. Like it asked me to put it to rest. This, like closing the physical space, was also an ending that brought grief later on. I just knew. I listened to the voice within me that isn't an asshole. The one that says, *It's okay to do this now. I don't know what's next for you, but you can end this thing and not hate yourself for it.*

That's the thing about choosing an end. You don't have to wait to know what's next. Maybe it is your style to love having something lined up. But the other thing about endings is, we don't always get to choose them. So we can practice ending things without being "ready" to train ourselves for the inevitable endings that are beyond our control.

o   o   o

OTHER PEOPLE'S ENDINGS THAT ARE NOW ALSO YOUR ENDING TOO

When John and I made the decision to end our marriage, it was really John's decision. We had been working together for a little under a year to figure out how/when/if we would end our partnership—sort of swinging back and forth between who needed what and who was more ready to say, *Okay, this is done now.*

So when it was time for John to REALLY be done, I was caught off guard. I think I thought that we had more time, that I had more time to be sure. I had thought I was sure and all set and ready to be done—but when I was suddenly sitting under a tree, on the third anniversary of our wedding day, staring at divorce papers—I thought, *Well, have we really done everything to try to save this thing that I don't even really want anymore but I can't imagine ending?*

In that moment, it became clear: it wasn't my ending—it was John's. John was clear on his ending. He had done his own searching within, he had made his own Venn diagrams and talked to his people, and he had done enough processing with me, to know it was time to end.

In Michigan, when you get divorced, they make you wait this grueling and very rude ninety days for it to be official. I know how long it takes to file a piece of paper, so I can only imagine this is some sort of Christian hoax to see if people will regret their decision to get divorced and miraculously decide to save said marriage.

Well, it worked on me. I went into a spiral that was so dark and so painful I honestly thought I would never emerge. I wanted to drink, I wanted to die, I screamed and cried into my rag rug in the back of Have Company after I asked John if he was sure and he said he wasn't in love with me anymore. I had never really considered that side of the ending, or that I too wasn't in love anymore. But hearing him say that, I thought certainly my life would end. This was it; this earth-shattering news would be the nail in my coffin. Throw me underground—there's nothing left.

Fast-forward to a month later. It was raining, and John called me after he left the courthouse where the divorce was finalized. I was cold to him, not because I wanted to be mean or make him feel bad, but because I didn't have anything left for him in that moment. We'd switched places: that day, the grief had locked in for him. It was really over: the paper was filed; the ending was in place. My ending happened after his ending, and then he had a new ending when it officially ended.

So, as you can see, one ending can have many chapters. And when the grief around the ending isn't shared, that can be just as painful as the ending itself.

This is the truth-telling. This is the reality. The story would have felt so pretty if we had just magically decided on the exact same day on the exact same moment that we were done in the exact same way. But it went through its own waves between us, together and individually.

Years later, this ending was our greatest gift. Our friendship and family ties are beyond the earthly plane. They are built on a cosmic foundation that weathers all things. And we would have never had that without the ending. This was a sunset, something that rose again.

A lot of this reminds me again of John's and my decision to move back in together at the end of 2018. This soft sunset like coming together. An ending that never really ended.

I also think about fear in this situation. The fear I felt when our marriage ended, the fear I felt when we moved back in together. *What if he brings someone home—will I feel jealous?*

Will I be unnecessarily rude and overprotective? Will we fight about the same stuff we fought about before?

We built a new container. And we did still fight about the same stuff we fought about before. But we found more creative ways to climb back out together. As friends who knew each other in a way only people who had been in a long-term romantic partnership could know each other. And then we invented a new thing. That's what happens when you end things: it means you get to invent new things. And reinvent them. And keep doing that over and over. It felt lucky in some ways. A mix of lucky and hard work.

But at the same time, it wasn't luck, it was that we accepted the ending. That it really was a sunset. It was soft and pink and blue and slow, and then it rose again!

o   o   o

YOU CAN SURVIVE AN ENDING

You can, I promise. I am certain of this. As a sober alcoholic, I have had the pleasure of being in the company of other sober alcoholics who have survived every single ending imaginable. Losing their homes, marriages, deaths of spouses, parents, and children, jobs, their own health's decline. And not only did they somehow manage to not drink or drug over it, they managed to survive the ending.

If me, a former blackout-binge-drinking, inconsiderate Gemini, can somehow manage to end a marriage and a dream space and leave the state she has always lived in and not only stay sober but also survive—you can too. You can have all the trauma in the world, and you can survive. I know this because you tell me.

I know this because I've seen it with my eyes and I have felt in my heart space and I have heard it with my own two ears. There is nothing that we cannot survive when something ends.

Part of the fear of surviving is when it's not up to you. When someone or the universe takes something from you. I find peace in the phrase "It wasn't yours to begin with." We get things to borrow, sometimes for a long time, sometimes for a short time.

My partner is in my sphere for now, so I do my best to take great care of this partnership. Because it deserves that right now, and because I don't get to choose how long its current state is a part of my truth.

The way my career is right now often feels both totally in my control and out of my control. I can research how to market and promote my work; I can send emails and reach out for opportunities, commit to daily writing and work, invest in myself and business, learn from my choices and see where I can get better.

But some seasons are just hard. No one emails back, half as many people sign up for an online class, something in my personal life takes hold, and I can't get a damn grip on my work. I get distracted and . . . well, there's a whole chapter on distraction.

Finding comfort in everything ending is also about being comfortable not knowing. Living one day at a time and knowing that literally anything could happen. You could even surprise yourself—that's half the fun. Start noticing when you end.

Also notice when you take breaks. Notice if you can start to find comfort.

Ending is different from finishing. And yet sometimes they are the same thing.

I might finish writing something, but it hasn't ended. I get to share it, read it, hold it, watch it expand others. I have this rug I've been working on for almost four years. Actually I worked on it for about a month and then a piece of it broke—it would take me approximately three minutes to fix this, but I haven't fixed it yet; I just carry it around to every place I've ever lived and it sits on the loom.

People often comment that the rug is indeed finished. I mean, it's been in this perpetual state for years; it just exists as a textile sculpture on a piece of wood. But I want so badly to finish it. Because I want to see the ending, the sunset, I want the painful process of becoming a finished object to end so I can share it in other ways. And so that I can use it. AND SO THAT I CAN START ANOTHER RUG. I DON'T EVEN KNOW WHAT RUG IS NEXT. The other route to take is to accept that it is actually time to just take it off the loom altogether, to release what the fabric has been carrying, thank it for its time on the pegs, and start anew.

The ending may seem insurmountable, planned or not. But we don't know what's next, and I keep finding that what's on the other side is sweeter than I could have ever thought up myself.

CHAPTER 4

On Not Knowing

Part of our endless fear of endings is not knowing how they will end. Will the ending be painful? Will it be traumatizing? And most important, will I survive it?

If I can access complete acceptance of the not knowing, I transition into ultimate joy. Into an ultimate state of being my full self, unattached to the outcome of the situation, or of my life, for that matter.

A simple practice I use daily is turning it over. Turning the outcome over and handing it back to the universe. You might hand it to God, to god, to goddess, to trees, to water, to air. But try handing it over to SOMETHING. Anything. It was never really yours to begin with—whatever situation you are in and whatever ending you are facing.

You can simply say: HERE YOU GO, UNIVERSE: YOU MAY DE-CIDE THE RESULTS NOW. My own will has barely gotten me anywhere. In fact, the more attached I am to an outcome, and an ending, a "final result," the more suffocated it becomes. The looser my grip, the freer it is to mutate into whatever it is supposed to be.

Another aspect of the unknown looms: If I did this thing once and it ended this way, if I try again, will it end the same way? I consider this going into any new relationship. But as I also contemplate *What if I ever wanted to get married again?* should I let the fear of how the first one ended stop me from trying again?

Not only did our vows not state that we would always be together, but I don't think I got married with the intention of growing old and dying with John. I loved him dearly, I loved to be his partner, but I was also twenty-four when that decision was made, and I thought: *If I get married, I can throw a big party and never go through a breakup again.* I have gone through seven more breakups since that decision. The party was very fun, though—I had a great time.

Making one decision does not prevent an ending of another situation. Nothing prevents us from pain, from endings, from death, or from dying ourselves. But we can continue to devote ourselves to the unknown and the mystery of our lives. And we can let it be sweet! We can let it be juicy! We can let it be pleasurable!

When a new romantic partnership begins, we open ourselves up in the same ways that didn't work before. How vulnerable! Even if we are vulnerable beings who can enter into the flow of love and communication naturally, old patterns start to emerge. We work through them; we grow stronger. But the closer we get, the more we must lean into the unknown, the fear of the ending, and the quality of our commitment.

I can shift this fear into acceptance. First, you choose to trust. You look at the facts—communication is solid, love is good, you feel seen, you feel confident in your future. But how many times have we all felt this and had a rug pulled out from underneath we never saw coming? A few, enough to have that little voice in our head that says, "You cannot trust this, and you cannot trust yourself, and you cannot trust this relationship, because everything ends!"

The only proof I have up until now is that every romantic relationship ends. But every relationship I have also been in has transformed into something more correct—something more beautiful. A few Christmases ago, I sat at my dining room table with two ex-partners, one of their fiancés, my brother, and both of my parents, who would later get divorced themselves after thirty-four years of partnership. Romantic relationships had transformed into something more in alignment, something we can all still take part in.

Everything ends. And then it becomes something else. And then something else is a new beginning and has a middle and also has an end. Sometimes the end is dying. Sometimes the end is the beginning of something else, and you can't tell the difference.

If we cannot withstand something, then it was never ours to withstand (turning it over). If our relationships end, we did not fail. We do not fall into a place of never deserving love again.

In my current partnership with Jackie, I often find myself saying, *Here you go, god—this one is for you. Jackie is yours, our love is yours, it's all yours. I will show up every day to do the work on myself and to grow this love, and maybe one day I*

will want to make a commitment that it is until I die, but for
now I just give it to you to do with what you think is best.

There is a part of not knowing that can also call us into deeper knowing. If I don't know something about myself, about how I walk through the world—it may be time to know it deeper. To seek teachers, books, resources that bring me into a greater knowing of myself.

SOMETIMES LEARNING AND knowing is uncomfortable at first—to see what you didn't know, what was hiding inside you. My inner critic is baffled at how I could go so long without knowing something so clear about myself.

Coming out was an extremely nonlinear process for me, as it is for many queers. As more time passes, and I lean more into myself and my sexuality, it comes with a certain harshness of myself, of *How could you not know? How could you not see this?*

I was in my early twenties the first time I publicly identified as queer. I had had sex with women, I knew I liked them, and I was still in complete denial that I had ever been in love with a woman. I had managed to fall in love, and to be physical—but never could match the two up.

Being queer doesn't have to have anything to do with who you have sex with. Plenty of cis folks in hetero-presenting relationships are queer—as was I! At twenty-nine years old, when I finally matched my love and physical intimacy with a woman, my mind sort of imploded. How could I not know? How could I have existed in the queer community and not known that this was here for me? How was I so filled with internalized homophobia that this was so terrifying to see?

I dug in everywhere—I found every lesbian history book I could get my hands on, I followed every Instagram account, I read every article. I had a whole history of myself I had never seen, I had never known.

I wondered, *If I had seen this—would I have known sooner?* If these histories were more visible—would I have seen myself sooner? The fear and disgust around women loving women is rampant in our society, in most societies. The idea that a man doesn't need to be present in a relationship threatens patriarchal ideas of what we "think" or are taught a family or partnership should look like.

My queerness brought me into another state of not knowing, and into more awareness around other forms of anti-oppression work. I started to see all of the other parts of my life and my identity and community I had fallen short on, and made a decision and choice to educate myself into a state of knowing.

In September of 2019 I took a long drive across the country with Jackie to move her to Michigan, and in the passenger seat I found myself feeling anxious and empty, thinking about the unknown, all the ways other relationships or friendships had gone wrong. I texted my friend and author Jen Pastiloff in this moment of *WHAT IS LIFE?* panic, and she reminded me of the beauty-hunting responsibility at hand.

All of a sudden, everything was a miracle. The shade of blue of a piece of machinery on the back of a semi, two horses' tails moving in unison next to a fence, the black-eyed Susans lining the highway, the day moon, the stacks of firewood at the campground in their perfect order, my best friend Katie coming home from Guitar Center and texting me a picture of her new cable, the SAME COLOR BLUE as on the semitruck.

It's so easy to forget that everything is a miracle, that beauty surrounds us in the most mundane, but it does, it does! Forgetting is a natural part of the process and remembering is the greatest gift. I knew then that the next season would hold so many unknowns. But I was also reminded that in seasons of great knowing—those truths are rooted in nothingness, and everything always changes. One thing I can rely on is my own ability to remember to OPEN MY EYES.

Also, nothing goes wrong (lol). OBVIOUSLY, things are just DIFFERENT WHENEVER THEY WANT TO BE.

Part of the reason I moved back to Michigan was to work on some DEEP inner patterns that I just couldn't quite access when I was in California. Money patterns, food, generosity, family dynamics. I wanted to set up systems for more ease and to see what was next.

"What is next" emerged! Then it got unclear again, and then I remembered it is always emerging. I would almost say effortlessly! And it's good to see how that ease comes from doing the most uncomfortable work of my life.

A lot of what I have to work on are my relentless habits and patterns I never thought I could break. Years of "messing up" making me feel so small. There is no messing up! Just different paces. And now that I am breaking through them, the relief is so sweet; the things I have been wanting to manifest are coming true.

Accessing joy without guilt, liking myself, loving my friends, new horizons, better digestion, acceptance of the dips, deeper attention, braver actions, brighter skin, perfect wrinkles, new people in my life transmuting their anger and despair into art and magic, a lot of god, all the plants, warm fleeces, strong hands, new sneakers, alive!

Okay, so I tell you all of this to maybe say KEEP IT MYSTERI-OUS. That is where the magic really is. In the not knowing. In the total and wild unknown of being alive. I'm in yet another zone of wanting to know how it ends—how does it turn out? What does all of this look like in ten years?! Attempting to fig-ure this out is so wasteful. MORE MYSTERY = MORE ACCEP-TANCE. Not knowing the ending can be the best part.

o   o   o

A PRAYER FOR COMING OUT

today i pray for magic
for glowing
for dykes and for fags everywhere

today i pray for softness
for listening
for queers and nonbinary people everywhere

today i pray for blooming
in gratitude for our ancestors
to do the work they started for us

today i pray to live true
to love every past self that brought me to this self

today i pray for lesbians and trans women of color
today i pray for the good fight
for rest and visible intimacy

today i pray you feel seen
no matter how you present
for feeling queer enough

today i pray for blissful love that catapults
through the air and into the everything

but more than ever ever ever i pray for safety, which
so many of us will never fully feel—but we can reach
toward together in an effort of ever flowing light

whether you've been out forever or you choose today
or tomorrow or the next day to come out, or maybe
you hate that "coming out" even exists and see its
problematic nature—i see you and i love you!

may all queers celebrate themselves today and
every minute—privately or publicly—partnered
or single—our visibility saves lives. some days it
feels better to normalize queerness, to see it as no
different from any other loving relationship—to self
or with others. but today i consider how my life
would have been different had i had more examples
of womxn loving womxn—would i have seen myself
sooner? if more trans and gender-nonconforming
folks felt safe in their visibility, would they have been
able to know themselves sooner? when we show

ourselves: others see themselves, what a gift.

but here's the thing—sooner isn't now, and there is no right timeline. may you love your whole self that brought you to where you are today. if you aren't ready to come out, that's okay—we'll be here with open arms ready to fold you in to the web of bold true magic.

CHAPTER 5

Asking for Help

You have to ask for help. This is not a suggestion or an opinion. This is the only way to do it. This is another truth I know. And I also am certain of its painful nature and how difficult it is for so many of us. Needing help assumes we are weak. That we cannot withstand pain on our own. I used to want to fight that—*I'll ask for help when I am a little bit stronger, a little more on my feet.*

The sooner I acknowledge my complete and total defeat around an ending, the sooner I can return to myself. Centering isn't about measuring how far away we are from the center and deeming us worthy of help or not. Asking for help is the fastest way for me to get to my center. It is the swiftest way for me to return, to not bury myself before I have a chance. Asking for help can be simple, it can be big, it can be soft, it can be angry. I sometimes ask myself for help by talking to my inner voice and saying, *Hi, Marlee, it's me, Marlee—I'm going to need some extra team backup on this one.* And if I can't access my inner voice, that is where I go to other humans, other resources, for help.

The Big Help

> Sit with your feet on the ground. Take a few deep breaths.
> What does your support team look like?
> What does your INNER support team look like?

In *How to Not Always Be Working*, I talk about my inner voice Roger, as Jen Pastiloff, who I mentioned before, talks about in her book *On Being Human*—the INNER ASSHOLE. Roger, even though I hate to admit this, is on my team. But he is not my whole team. Roger came to me in a craniosacral session while I was in a sort of trance state. I was facing my inner critic, and it was so loud. In that moment I needed a name for it, and I blurted out ROGER.

But, if I have Roger, which my mind invented, then I must also be able to willingly invent other characters in the scene. So at some point, I invented Gloria. Gloria wears a pantsuit a lot like Bette Porter on *The L Word*. She takes calls, she makes plans, she runs the show. She's beautiful, she loves herself, and she is very good at telling Roger to sit down. She tells Roger: *Thank you so much for showing up to the meeting, but we're gonna take it from here!*

That's the thing about your inner shitty voice—you don't have to yell at it or banish it forever. You can simply say: *Hi. I see you.* It's another part of you that so desperately wants to be seen. To be acknowledged for all the effort it's given to work so hard and not be seen or heard. Roger isn't just my inner mean voice: Roger is the voice that says, *You have tried this and failed so many times; why would you ever try again?*

Which brings me to the idea of enoughness, about the ways we might feel broken or whole, and remind you this book is for everyone—no matter where you are on the spectrum of feeling like your complete self.

I have a bit of a hot take that I've had mixed reviews on, alas—I shall present it to you anyway in an effort to give you something to either wholly accept or push back against with all your strength. I have seen both reactions cause greater trust with self.

There's a kind of saying in yoga classes and in the self-help world—I've probably written it in a newsletter or something somewhere. There are entire books about it, and people say it to you and they text it to you when you're sad. They say, "You are enough. You are enough."

Maybe we stop saying that. Here's why:

Maybe you're not enough, and that's fine. You can still love yourself even if you're "not enough." I've experienced the "not-enough-ness" often. Partly because I want to get better. Maybe you're not enough, and that's cool. You can still like yourself for not being enough and actively work to be a better person in the world. If I really believed I was enough, I would just quit. I'd say, *Oh . . . well, now that I'm enough, what's left?*

Again, this phrase works SO WELL for so many people. It keeps them from killing themselves! It helps them wake up in the morning! But this new idea is actually working GREAT for me; instead of every day saying, "I'm enough, I'm enough just the way I am," I say, "No, I have some really serious stuff I'm working on, and wanna work through and wanna improve at." I also like myself IN that. I like Marlee that's in process.

If you feel like you're not enough, that's fine. I'm going to love myself in the not-enough-ness. Because every day, whether it's scrolling my feeds, checking my email, getting a text or not getting a text, or seeing somebody do something awesome, and I get that little feeling where I think, *I'm not enough*, well, yeah, maybe I'm not. And that's fine.

I share this tangent of thought because I think it fits nicely into the realm of asking for help. As soon as I think I'm enough, I forget to ask. I mean, I do think I am PERFECT JUST THE WAY I am TODAY. And then I do a little inventory to see where I could use some extra help to benefit my growth.

HELP COMES IN all forms, and I also want to talk about prayers and archetypes.

Friend and pastor Cindy Pincus recently shared with me about the archetype of a psychopomp, a spiritual guide who helps people across rivers or to other spirit worlds. I was able to connect with this vision, to search examples in history and mythology about psychopomps and see where they fit into my own work. Asking for help can be spiritual; in fact, I think it *should* be spiritual.

This doesn't have to mean god/God/religion by any means. But a blade of grass, the waves, the awe that comes with asking divine source for a little extra guidance.

Asking for help from our ancestors, creating altars, this is what we can build off of—especially when accessing human connection feels like it is too much or too overwhelming.

When I am feeling resistant to my own art making or writing, I return to these words by Toni Morrison in regards to how civilizations heal when the world is bruised and bleeding:

"This is precisely the time when artists go to work. There is no time for despair, no place for self-pity, no need for silence, no room for fear. We speak, we write, we do language."—Toni Morrison

ANY TIME MERCURY is stationed in retrograde, I have an opportunity to learn a lot about the BENEFITS of the mess, about what going to work means to me and how to share it clearly and truly. I can get caught in a shame spiral around my commitment to vagueness, and I can also step up to see how it affects those I love. I take an inventory and see where I owe professional amends. I spent four weeks worrying about something that took me thirty minutes. I can receive amazing news and decide I didn't deserve it.

I share all of this to now tell you how I emerge, that it isn't magic—it is really, really hard work, and digging myself all the way to the bottom to come back up, I truly have to "act my way into right thinking."

But there can also be magic with the tangible help. One particularly hard retrograde, I had my friend and artist Whit Forrester come over, and we built a huge altar in the attic, and that was magic. Always both.

○ ○ ○

(OTHER WAYS I ASK FOR HELP)

Text my mentor for advice
Call into a recovery meeting
Get on the phone with a sponsor
Go for a walk
Drink a ton of water
Hire a bookkeeper FOR THE FIRST TIME EVER and
don't let Roger sabotage this small victory
Take my daily herbal tincture even
after I skip it for a few days
Call my little brother back
Schedule a craniosacral session
FaceTime a friend
Send an amends email for not showing
up when I committed
Open up some old mail
Make a mixtape
Read my horoscope

○ ○ ○

IT'S HAS BECOME SO CLEAR to me that nothing outside of myself can make me feel BETTER OR WORSE. This is a breakthrough, but I am definitely seeing where even the BEST NEWS EVER leaves me thinking, *Damn, I am still just me*, and how much inner work I have to do to love myself. While asking for help is essential—asking for help should also be seen as a tool for strengthening our inner abilities to build self-worth—oftentimes when I am seeking help outside of myself there is a crack in my self-esteem. Other times it's physical pain, mental health issues—but even those—I feel myself start to beat myself up for even having to ask for help, which chips away at my self-worth.

I write and talk a lot about ritual, devotion to self, and how I forgive myself when I don't keep those promises. As I sat down to write one morning, on the new moon, I asked myself some questions to look at the cycles, waves, and tides of commitment keeping/not keeping—without judgment.

It's easy to sink into internet validation to ignore a lack of self-validation/faithfulness to self. While I generally post for my own documentation/research, I would be lying if I said I wasn't CURIOUS about the receptivity of a Personal Practice post. I mean I could just do things alone and never show you, but there's something in the showing. It makes me feel connected, it's fun, it's part of my work to share.

But if that sort of mass showcasing isn't linking up with relentless devotion to self and real-life community, I start feeling extremely empty.

o   o   o

HERE IS A list of questions I asked myself in the Spring of 2019.

You can use these questions yourself, or build in your own inventory-taking practice to see where and to whom you might reach out for help

What have I been obsessing over?

I ask myself this because generally anything I am obsessing over I am putting before god

Did I drink water?

No, usually, is the answer if I have to ask

Where is the moon today?

New, the light will return, I return to myself

What day of my cycle was it when ____ happened?

Well, when I hated everything it was day twenty-five because that's always what happens on day twenty-five, so now I can take stock and look ahead

Did I pray that day?

Probably not, but you can always pray at any moment—you can always be in prayer; I am typing this and praying

Is there someone I haven't called back?

Yes, or there is someone I can call, email, be of service to

Did I future pace myself?

This is where I generally miss a commitment. If I always write my newsletter on a Monday morning but I am spending a Monday morning driving through a blizzard just to kiss a girl, then I should probably write my newsletter that Saturday before—FUTURE PACING/DAYS CHANGE

What is future pacing?! Future pacing is looking ahead

at what other commitments, social events, and work things you have coming up. You can then track other parts of your life. Where are you in your menstrual cycle? What phase will the moon be in? What season is it outside?

For example, if someone asks me to do something that involves being public and I know it will fall on a new moon that also happens to be the day I start bleeding that also happens to come after two other big commitments—I would choose to FUTURE PACE and say no. And remember, "no" is a complete sentence.

Have I eaten a vegetable in the last four days?

I probably have, but do I REMEMBER THE VEGETABLE?

Am I stretching?

No . . .

How fast can I forgive myself for not doing these things?

FASTER! WRITING THIS IS HELPING!

Have I been alone without my phone for more than an hour?

DID I JUST MOVE ACROSS THE ENTIRE COUNTRY BACK TO A PLACE WHERE I GOT SOBER/A LITERAL BLOCK AWAY FROM WHERE I WAS BORN/WAS MARRIED TO SOMEONE IN/MY PARENTS LIVE/IT'S LITERALLY COVERED IN FEET OF SNOW AND I CAN'T SWIM OUTSIDE?

Okay, so the last question on that list was dramatic, but the answer is yes. BUT—not to be some sort of hard-ass coach to myself, this is good information. However, with this information comes action—without action, without doing the next right thing—I'm in my bed for four hours staring at my phone and making my eyes go blurry.

My eyes started blurring out in the fall of 2018, and I'd been ignoring it, hoping that it would just go away. What a sweet metaphor for everything else. I finally took myself to an eye doctor. At first I was so mad at myself, but then my inner voice was like, *YES, YOU DID IT! You got what you need to SEE! Thank you so much for helping us see—this is going to be so great.*

The thread that goes through each of these questions is the *What am I obsessing over?* question. This is generally where I can start to rearrange, take apart, add on. Obsession comes in all forms—the unbridled joy of new love, the debilitating pain of grief and loss, the unending fear of fucking up or not being good enough.

In order to rearrange, I start a conversation with my inner voice, who I mentioned before takes on many forms. Roger, Gloria, the inner wounded Marlee around age nine.

We have been really going at it, me and the inner voice. Me and the little versions of Marlee. She is so loud and really knows best, and to be honest she isn't wrong, but she totally forgets I have a body that bleeds and bends and sleeps and thinks. But now that we're working together, it's going a lot better.

We (me and inner me/highest self me) review the above questions together. Untie, cut, chop, slice, add on to the never-ending quilt that is a day, a week, a season, a chapter. And then it's lighter. We're just trying things out. And if they don't go the way we originally planned, then what a blessing to see what's new and what's next, and so far the last thirty years have shown me that there is so much magic around every corner if I just get my blurry eyes checked and keep them wide open.

o o o

A PRAYER FOR ASKING FOR HELP

*A totally made-up spell I love to say in my head over
and over is BLESSINGS ABOUND, BLESSINGS ABOUND.
It helps me when I am anxious, when I just don't know
what the hell to do. When there is no clear pathway to
or from center in sight. I just say it over and over and
I almost always calm down a bit. That even though
outside help is so important, my connection with
the divine and myself is the one thing that is always
there—steadfast and true. It's my way of asking
the universe for help in a quick and direct way.*

CHAPTER 6

Devotion

Devotion, prayerful observance, and unconditional love. For the self, for a task, for another. Devotion is as risky as it gets. To be wholly devoted is to lose part of yourself. As Mary Oliver said, "Attention is the beginning of devotion."

To be devoted—to be disciplined, we become disciples to ourselves. We become champions of paying attention.

In this place of risk—what are we willing to lose? Self-protection and care—not to protect us from what is within, but protecting us from the hardships of the world—is also part of what makes devotion risky.

It is important to remember that living under the heteronormative white supremacist patriarchy creates so much harm, that our devotion practice is both asking to be dialed up, as well as protected from so many forces that are against so many of us.

We build practices. We become wholly, wildly, boundlessly devoted. To ourselves and to our practices that we have visioned and to the people we love. This devotion radiates out into the rest of the world. And we do this knowing that keeping this devotion is a gamble. Because the world takes things away, or we walk away, or something—continually we can count on—will knock us off our center.

What IS devotion to you? What does being devoted without losing yourself really look like?

I encourage you to meditate on using the word "no" as saying "yes" to yourself. I have the word "yes" tattooed on my right hand, and I used to worry people would assume I had a really hard time saying no. But this tattoo faces me—it's a reminder to keep saying yes to myself. Keep saying yes to being alive. And this often means saying no to other people and to plans.

Part of staying devoted to myself is this practice—of saying no, placing boundaries, and carving out space for myself to stay devoted to my visions for a practice. To what keeps me in the center.

Devotion to community, and to our work, to the things we love. Devotion to help us endure pain and hardship that surrounds us either right on time or totally unexpectedly. We are called to show up for this. Building a team of others who help you stay accountable, who provide mirrors of seeing yourself, who ask YOU for your advice and guidance.

Community devotion also casts a wide net to those who you might be of service to, your real-life communities and your online communities. Usually when I see a topic, a news story, a thread of urgency emerge on social media, I pause. I ask myself—what people or organizations in the current community I live in are already doing this work, and what can I do to lift up their work, their voices, and donate monetarily? If the issue at hand doesn't have a reference point outside of its exact formation, you may want to pay attention to what your collaborators, peers, or other public people you look toward are doing in terms of action.

PART OF DEVOTION is also turning toward the self, rather than turning toward distraction.

In times of computer focus, I CAN choose not to open a new browser. I can rearrange my words to proclaim that I CAN instead of *I should*, or *I want to*, or *I wish I could*. I CAN do things differently. Saying to myself, *I really shouldn't open the new browser*, isn't particularly helpful.

The way we speak to ourselves, communicate with the many inner dialogues we may have going at any time, is to practice this devotion to ourselves. Part of this is that we CAN be nice to ourselves. And to also be aware of where we already practice great devotion to the self, even when we start building in narratives that we do not.

I consider my best friend and musician Katie Crutchfield to be one of my many coaches on creative devotion. In the process of writing or working on big projects, I build narratives that I am undisciplined, not devoted, and sabotage my process. When I shared this with her, she gently reminded me of all the many things I have stayed wholeheartedly devoted to.

To staying sober, sending out my newsletter every week, to Jackie, to the process of learning about attachment theory, to the work to undo ancestral trauma. I have indeed stayed very devoted to many things.

But my mind can quickly decide that if there is one part of getting knocked off center, every single part may as well go in the trash.

Hopefully little sparks are flying around your beautiful brain as you read this! Because like most of what I say, I believe that if it can be true for me it can be true for you. Feeling a lack of devotion in one aspect of your life—YOU ARE NOT A TRAGIC LOSS TO SOCIETY!

Make a list—make a list of all the things you HAVE been able to stay devoted to. This could be as simple as flossing or as grand as going for a walk three times a week for twenty years. Honestly, both are huge wins in my book. Only you get to make the barometer for your devotion. This is part of your devotion to getting to center.

DEVOTION AND DISTRACTION go hand in hand, so before we get to distraction, I want to talk more about how the devotion to self is going to be our strongest armor against the great knowns and unknowns trying to take us as far away from the self as possible.

The world can be against us. Not in a teen angst way where we decide every system is shit and trying to take us down and there is nothing good in the world, but the fact that in 2020 we are amidst the greatest levels of distractions we have ever seen. How do stay with ourselves through this? Devotion.

Whether it is an advertisement on TV, the way our screens draw us in, the fact that there is always some better, faster, stronger product to heal us—what is at the root of our center is our devotion.

The distractions that we often reach for cause an immediate low. It is not fun. There is an immediate feeling of failure, of sabotage. The noise. How much we are consuming. And how we actually cannot hear anything. But I also want to point out how we can use pathways of distraction and reroute them into devotional roadways for the self and for others.

Let's take social media for example. What if we started casting spells around our use of Instagram, Twitter, even Tinder if you're swiping? I'm always digging into this relationship. As an addict, I think I always will be. I want to reach for it, all the time. I always want to leave my body. Leave whatever I am doing.

I hold two waves of thoughts. One is *stay*. When you want to reach, just stay. Stay an extra moment in whatever feeling you are having, whatever thing you are doing, just stay a little bit longer.

And the other is to bring a mindful spirit to the next action. Okay, so you are going to reach for your phone. It's happening. You are going to open the scroll. How do we do it with reverence and joy. With the intention to bring peace and harmony to every post we consume and every post we make.

At this point, you might be thinking, *This is nuts*. There is nothing reverent or spiritual about a social media app. WELL, MY FRIEND, you're on it all day and can't seem to step away, so maybe it's time to think otherwise. Maybe it's time to make everything a prayer.

Becoming a dog mom was something that brought me more into my aliveness and consciousness. More into the parts of myself that were in need of more attention paying, devotion to having my eyes open. Especially having a puppy, all eyes have to be on her at all times, or she could really get hurt. If she gets into something because I am not paying attention to her, I might have to chase her or get something out of her mouth or go find her if she's run off—which naturally aggravates my nervous system and gets me all out of sorts.

So if I can be fully devoted to paying attention to her, I not only see more of the world—I also see more of her, more of myself, less strung out.

○ ○ ○

CLARITY AS DEVOTION TO SELF

I am grateful to be rooted in the truth. I see how my vagueness in actions and communication can affect those around me, and it is important to note that clarity brings me back to my center. Clarity is an act of devotion—specifically because it is born out of avoidance and fear.

There have been times where I am working on longer projects that a few days of avoidance can spin into a deadly month—many months; even years—of avoidance.

This, this cycle of nonforgiveness, IS deadly. I don't use this word lightly—for it is my true belief that by not carving out the time and space for our practice, we can get sick. Our bodies start to hurt, we become disillusioned, our joys are outweighed by the guilt of not showing up to ourselves.

But we can forgive ourselves. Usually when I come back home from a trip away, whether it is a few days or a few weeks, my transition time is very difficult. I meet this resistance not because the days are actually hard, but because I push against what my body and mind actually need.

In discovering what I am devoted to—it is that I am devoted to going at my own pace—without guilt or shame. And DAMN, is that hard. Especially with the facts as I mentioned before that we are going through life inundated with suggestions, products for being better, examples of other people's lives that don't seem to include much rest.

Time away from a partner/home life to devote time to self and creativity is magic, but sometimes the coming back to reality can be especially jarring. You have to get used to cocreating again, having favors asked of you just as you were about to do something for yourself.

ANOTHER REQUIREMENT FOR devotion to love is utter devotion to self. If I start to skimp on the things that bring me closer to my own truth, my devotion within the partnership starts to feel thin and rusty.

Complete and absurdly paralyzing avoidance usually comes when there is something waiting to get out of me. My guides are begging me to sit down to write.

Fear—of success, of coming into my power, of sharing my gifts, of selfishly wanting to play all day—takes over. And self-forgiveness is a faraway thought I can't seem to grasp onto.

Alas, that is the answer over and over again. I commit to writing. It might seem counterintuitive to use these pages to explain to you how I got to them in the first place. But I think that's what the book is about: how you do one thing is how you do everything.

o   o   o

FINANCIAL DEVOTION

Part of my path with devotion has been to look at what is making me feel unsafe in regards to my money habits.

Healing ancestral trauma and habits around money has been more of a one-step-forward-three-steps-back journey for me. But holy smokes, does that make the one step forward feel like the greatest thing ever.

Growing up middle-class to parents who wanted to provide so much for us, leaning into credit cards and going into debt, created habits and narratives within myself. Not just from my family but from those I surrounded myself with—punks, queers, struggling artists.

Some beliefs include but are not limited to:

o Rich people are bad
o People who have money are bad
o People who go on nice vacations are rich people, and we don't do that—we go camping
o Buying things makes us feel better
o We have to present one way because if we present a different way we will look poor
o Why would we try to save or budget when we can hardly keep up

It was bad to be rich, but it was good to look sort of rich. We can't keep up, so why get clarity on how much is going in or out? And more inherited beliefs that are no one's fault but have now been handed to me to do with what I will.

Money stuff is A LOT! It is one of the greatest causes of shame and self-loathing because, even though most of us were never taught what a healthy and clear relationship with money looks like, we are so mad at ourselves for not KNOWING BETTER.

I have found that many artists and writers in their thirties like myself are facing this truth without many resources. And while I am often in the three-steps-back category of learning this—I would like to share some of what I know from the one-step-forward movement of my life:

- It's okay if you currently do not understand how money works
- It is going to take time; these habits and mindsets are from many generations back and have a grasp not just on your thinking but on your DNA
- We can be generous with money! Having money is not bad
- Saving money is not bad
- When we learn how to do all of this, we get to share it with others

One of the greatest days of my life (honestly) was when I showed a friend how to log into Credit Karma. He had been avoiding it for literally years, assuming his credit was so embarrassingly bad that he didn't even want to look at it. We logged in, and that shit was over seven hundred. For YEARS, he had assumed the absolute worst, when indeed it was not only a good credit score, but the things against it were now clearly listed and easy to address!

I have been working to grow my unimpressive credit score, and this has been a devotional act: to make calls to creditors, get right with my student loans, open up a secured credit card, actually pay it on time, set up QuickBooks, and just do the damn thing. Checking my bank account even when it is scary. Even when I have reverted YET AGAIN to manic spending habits to avoid saving. Because only comfortable people save, and being comfortable is a privilege that I don't want to have.

Here is the thing that isn't cool about that, though. Having the privilege to make money and then to spend it wastefully is exactly how we use our privilege in incorrect ways. Guilt around our privilege, whether it is about our race, sexuality, class, or otherwise—does not lead us into restorative action. It leads us into actions that are not in alignment with our values.

Saving and making money can be a creative and devotional act. It can be a way to vision a new future or present for yourself and for others that you believe in. This, again, is about getting to the other side of the river. When it comes to financial devotion, I ask for a lot of help, and usually when I stop asking for help is when I am in the three-steps-back zone.

Our dedication to clarity around money, to not underearning, to leaving vagueness, is going to open up so many new doors for all of us. More doors mean more opportunities means more healing means more of us in our centers—so that when we get knocked off, financial clarity can be something we look at and say: *Hello, I see you.*

My time in Michigan was really dedicated to releasing old money habits and creating new ones. One thing I noticed was how I felt really confident and maybe I was on track and then heard about a big number I had to pay that I hadn't expected.

It reminds me again that only vagueness can lead me to feeling "okay" or safe. This is a false sense of safety. Only clarity can provide us real safety—and even then we live in a GROUND-LESS world where anything could happen. Instead of hiding or reaching for distraction or whining, I am looking the numbers clearly in the eye and asking for help.

"Money Madness brings despair. We feel we will never get ahead. Solvency breeds hope. We see the light at the end of the tunnel. Our dignity returns."

—JULIA CAMERON

One way to do this is writing the numbers down. You could have a little notebook and every single day write down every penny that you spend. The act of tracking it keeps you in clarity rather than vagueness. There are tools like QuickBooks. For many of you, a simple spreadsheet could do. Writing out upcoming expenses, writing in how much you're spending a month on groceries or clothes. Opening up your bank account when you're scared. Although there are certainly a lot of factors that can add to money scarcity, no matter where you are in your process I believe that just adding a little bit of willingness to find clarity is a great start.

CHAPTER 7

Distraction

When I look at myself on a daily basis, when I look at what I really want from being alive, the one thing that almost always gets in my way are distractions. Distractions take us away from our commitments, our devotion to self.

But can distractions serve us? Can we find a way to see our distractions as tiny gifts—floating into our sphere to teach us what we really want to say, letting ourselves love them every once in a while?

My favorite no-shame distraction is television. I will never shame a single person or myself for watching a television show. And I'm not talking about only accepting the beautiful cinematic new HBO show or some docuseries about the world changing. I am talking trashy, prime-time TV that's only purpose in life is to entertain and distract you.

EAT IT UP. Take it all. Eat every bit of the cake that is your favorite TV show. If you're at hour six of watching in one day, maybe we step away from the screen. But also, MAYBE we

DON'T.

Distractions often serve to protect us, to keep us safe. Little blankets of comfort for our overworked minds. This kind of distraction often calms my mind much more than the phone screen or the social media scroll. I can sit back, relax, take in my story, maybe eat a snack that I love. I am relaxed; I am on a fictional journey that is not my own life. And often this quieting of my mind can lead me back to the other things that bring me joy or productivity.

A lot of our aversion to pleasure is guilt around rest, which we'll address later.

THEN THERE IS the greatest distraction of them all. The one I write about all the time, the one I dig myself out of time after time. The app. The photo and video social networking service, Instagram. Built like a slot machine for the human soul, the soul that can be crushed by the never-ending dopamine loop.

I know what you're thinking: *Wouldn't it be nice if we could all run away from the internet forever? Never look again. Never have to deal with the scroll addiction and the shame that follows. Never compare and despair.*

But—what a tool! And dropping out carries its own problematic new truth: we lose the responsibility to our neighbors and ourselves and the ability to reach people to change the world.

How can we do both? A question many writers and artists and critics are asking themselves and their audience, myself included.

I continue to seek other writers asking these questions and

offering new solutions, new futures. I want us to build them together. While reading Jia Tolentino's *Trick Mirror: Reflections on Self-Delusion*, this stuck out to me: "I've been thinking about the five intersecting problems—first, how the internet is built to distend our sense of identity; second, how it encourages us to overvalue our opinions; third, how it maximizes our sense of opposition; fourth, how it cheapens our understanding of solidarity; and finally, how it destroys our sense of scale."

There seems to be an overwhelming shame in sharing ourselves and our findings, in self-promotion. We get caught up in the frenzy and the crisis level of posting and sharing and ENGAGING—a made-up responsibility that keeps us in fear and anxiety—rather than in a nourished state of inspiration and sharing from a place of magic and abundance.

WE *MUST STAY COMMITTED TO THE DAILY MAINTENANCE OF OUR LIVES *OFF* THE SCREEN TO SHARE OUR FINDINGS AT A SLOW AND NONURGENT PACE!!! TO STAY IN RATHER THAN DROP OUT!*

SO, with this distraction, and like many distractions—we also understand that they are tools. Most things that I reach for as distractions also serve a nourishing and beautiful purpose in my life. This is part of why it is painful to let them become distractions.

Food, sex, social media, shopping, TV shows, socializing: all are things that I like. They are all things that fuel me and fill me up and make me happy inside. They could also all be on the list of things that distract me.

Part of me wonders after looking at this list if maybe it's time to shift what a distraction even is. The definition for a distraction is a thing that prevents someone from giving full attention to something else.

So, as a centering practice, we check in. We build in pauses throughout the day. Some might call it a mindfulness practice. I just call it a *Hey, what the hell is going on up there in my head?* practice. If I'm feeling relaxed and sure, I might not call for a check-in. But if I am about to rip my girlfriend's clothes off after being struck by a pang of crippling anxiety and not-enoughness, I have an opportunity to ask myself why and close the gap on what to do the next time it happens. Sex as a distraction and attachment mechanism vs. sex as a moment to connect. With all of this, there isn't a right or wrong. It's just about turning up the dial of noticing.

Is there some big other commitment to self I said I would do today that I am avoiding?

Is this intimacy my distraction because I don't want to face myself?

Is this intimacy a pivot moment where I get to relax and find pleasure with someone I love before returning to my work?

DING DING DING—I am LOVING THAT LAST QUESTION

Okay, so this is where we get to start seeing our "distractions" as little gifts of what our priorities are, and then letting them include rest and recharging activities!

I think we paint distractions as such terrible things because we are also attaching heaping piles of judgment to them. That is not actually helpful; it's just adding to the spiral. Or, my favorite story to tell myself: I am an easily distracted person and that is just the way I am. I mean, it kind of is just the way I am. But I am learning and teaching myself new ways of pausing and exercising these feelings around STAYING.

What if we stayed in something a little longer than was comfortable? What if we stayed with it past the one or two moments of wanting to reach for the phone or just quit altogether? I let myself have a few moments of wanting to quit, and then by the third or fourth I might lean into that feeling and let myself pause, with full permission to return to it when and if I want to.

o o o

ON HOPING SOMETHING FIXES US

Or, why we keep reaching.

I notice a common thread when people review *How to Not Always Be Working* on Amazon or Goodreads—they say, "This wasn't life-changing, but . . . ," and then they list approximately five to thirteen ways it completely changed their lives. . . .

I want to remind you, and myself, that nothing can fix us. What does it mean to have your life changed? A good piece of French toast can change my life. A wink, the way birds fly together.

I think our lives are always changing, but we have these unattainable expectations for what that looks like—my online class can't fix you; neither can this book, or my last book. I think that distraction is a way we think this will get fixed in us. I hope to provide tools for subtle shifts and waking up. And for you to notice the small ways things change you every damn day!

That's the thing we are always changing. This is one of the reasons I am so often drawn to distractions. Because I haven't trained myself in the habit of just sitting with it. Just sitting in the discomfort. Letting go of guilt that comes with discomfort.

Narratives around "not having it as bad as someone else"—no matter what the topic is—are an example of how I can sometimes distract myself from my feelings. And then, instead of facing our pain, we reach for a distraction. This is where I do not think distractions serve us. They may keep us safe, but they aren't serving us. They may soothe us, but they aren't teaching us. And that's okay! You can go at your own pace. But I have found time and time again that the best way for me to really take my blooming and growing to the next level is by facing my pain. Not minimizing it because I think, *This shouldn't hurt me so much.*

The best way to heal what is broken or needs fixing—or, if you hate those phrases, "needs tending to"—is to sit with it. To sit still, or to dance to Plantasia and find movement. To put on your favorite pop album and dance it out and then follow it up with a silent walk or ten minutes of silent sitting.

I love the seasons of my life where I am really committed to taking myself on walks. I try to find the inner part of me that is in obsession (obsession is my other favorite mode of distracting myself from the right now), and I just ask it what it needs. What does obsessed Marlee need? What didn't she get as a kid? How can she be soothed and brought into her power now?

These conversations or silent sits with myself have brought

me closer to my center, one day at a time. And I make friends with the distractions that still come up.

They aren't quick fixes. Distractions are often quick fixes, though—that's why we love them. I don't mean to paint intimacy with a romantic partner as some kind of bad thing; in fact, if you're getting that, thank the whole freaking goddess. But I know, for me, I can see when it's coming from place of wanting to fill a void that might be better filled from turning inward and not from a place of wanting true intimacy.

Now, I have also been in seasons of my life where fast, casual sex is sort of like my suggestion for feeling no shame around watching your favorite TV show. Like all things I suggest, they are specific to me in this season of my life. As long as your actions are safe and feeling awesome, I have zero opinion on them. I have zero opinion on them if they're not feeling awesome either, but the point of all of this is for you to apply the tools as they are specific to your own life.

o   o   o

DISTRACTIONS: ENDLESS JOY
AND INTERNAL DISCORD

My life experience is in fact the research and the root and the revelations that are held in these pages. I am easily distracted. It is my constant uphill battle to reimagine my life on a daily basis to see how to be more present—to live fully and to live with rigor and vitality and not REACH, REACH, REACH. While internal discord is often my reason for reaching for the distraction, one I've been able to pinpoint more easily, I'm now in a season where joy and love can be just as dangerous, pulling me away from my current reality.

o   o   o

Here's the sequence that depletes me:

> *I feel a big feeling*
> *I want what I want right now*
> *I can't have that thing*
> *I look at Instagram (no metabolization, just*
> *empty-god-sized-hole-filling scrolling)*
> *That makes me feel bad*
> *I find a new distraction*
> *Repeat pattern*

Here's the sequence that nourishes me:

> *I feel a big feeling*
> *I want what I want right now*
> *I can't have that thing*
> *I pour a glass of water and I drink that water*
> *That makes me feel good*
> *I want to reach for my phone; I do not*

Instead I open my computer to pour myself into my writing or my online class. I can also choose to draw, sew, or call a friend.

o   o   o

IT SEEMS THAT in these times of phone reaching, it is really a quiet fear that I am not good enough to write, to sew, to be a person.

In order to tap into the bright prism of my life I have also found that I need to take breaks. Sometimes these breaks I really have to work for. Sometimes I speak them into existence and the divine source helps me keep them true. I mentioned being single in 2019 for a few months, which for some people might sound like a lifetime and for others might feel like nothing. For me it was much longer than I had gone in almost a decade, and it was transformative, eye-opening, amazing to have no distractions. I mean, I had some—I am not immune to crushes or the text of a past lover reeling me in. But to not be in pursuit, to have no physical romantic contact, was a huge gift that opened me up to a new sense of self I hadn't known I would get to uncover.

Now, within partnership, I try to access some of that same distraction-free sentiment while not being single. Taking trips away from our home to visit a friend, doing an artist residency, committing deeply to my own hobbies and career so as to not lose myself. Sometimes—I hate to admit this; it hurts me—I see my whole relationship turning into one big distraction. But it is also really important for me to admit that to myself, because it's a sign it's time to get back to my center. I want to be my own center, and to see my partner have her center. Those centers can then intersect like a Venn diagram, but if we aren't careful they just become one circle and we lose ourselves.

So I leave, I take a trip, we make sure to have our own individual days even if we are both working from home all day.

We talk openly about the ways codependence and attachment styles show up in our relationship, we are honest when we need alone time and personal space, and we don't take it personally.

o   o   o

MEDIA DISTRACTION

I want to offer an entry point to thinking about consuming less media, the benefits of the mute button, that it's okay to not look—even at your dearest friend or inspiration.

The antidote to overconsumption of art and images and feeds and everything coming at you is creation: to turn the phone off and get tangible or messy, to keep writing, to sit at the sewing machine, to go outside, to swim, to be with friends, to chop a vegetable, to return to daily habits lost.

If you're feeling like you can't metabolize everything coming at you, see what you can do to consume less and create more, without tying your creativity/output to your worth—it's a doozy. I'm trying; we can try at this together.

We turn to our actions. If a magnetic and wild new love IS distracting you and pulling you from your center, return to your visions for a practice. What keeps you there, what brings you back—and how do you ACTUALLY feel the love in your body, not just the idea of love?

For me, falling in love is my most extreme case of losing myself. I will stray so far away from my center of self, center of gravity, there is nothing left. I am in a total cosmos of love obsession and am convinced that nothing can bring me back—so why even try?

The *Why even try?* question is my self-sabotage. My inner voice loves to remind me of how often I can let love spin me out, that I cannot manage to act in different ways. This gives us two options, which can be accepted simultaneously.

This is the way I am, fast to fall in love. To see the magic in another and how it reflects back to me. And I can also pause more; I can shift the actions. The pulsing in my veins and my mind and my spirit may be the same until I die. But I can transmute this into reality—something I once wasn't able to do.

I am not perfect at this, but slowing down and entering into a state of spaciousness seems to help.

In Kahlil Gibran's *The Prophet*, he speaks of partnership:

> *Give your hearts, but not into each other's keep-*
> *ing.*
> *For only the hand of Life can contain your hearts.*
> *And stand together, yet not too near together:*
> *For the pillars of the temple stand apart,*
> *And the oak tree and the cypress grow not in*
> *each other's shadow.*

It is this spaciousness that I long for. To grow in my own light, not in the shadow of another. To pull into my own roots, alongside another. This is true not just in romance, but in platonic intimacy as well.

I find that by cultivating platonic intimacy, my ability to withstand the off-centeredness of falling in and out of love is less tumultuous, less chaotic. I don't claim to want to love any differently, but I want the world around me to turn upside down less. To affect the ones closest to me less.

It takes a lot of the tools I write about here to stay with myself, to not abandon myself in feelings of being unwanted or unlovable. While I began writing this book unpartnered, it seems the book writes itself. Within a week of beginning the book, I met Jackie, my skateboard got stolen, I was living with my ex-husband, my parents told me they were getting divorced, and I received a whirlwind of character assassination criticism.

Yet I still sat down write. I drank my water. I took deep breaths, and I kept starting over again. I would have maybe preferred to navigate these, or any variety of task, within a partnership.

I think this is where we can be shortsighted. In my time of being single, I found myself more partnered than ever before. While we glorify being single as the "necessary thing" to do in between partnerships (something I have always scoffed at), I saw in that moment where it allowed me to grow into myself, in a way I couldn't before—in the loops of falling in and out of love so often and so quickly.

I'd be hesitant to call them nonromantic partnerships. They are nonsexual, but they are deeply intimate. They are filled with romance. Flights to visit each other, photo-booth photos, flowers sent, front-row sing-alongs—every ounce of me has butterflies when I see these friends.

These people, the ones that I trust and love unconditionally, nourishing these relationships, keeps me right within.

o   o   o

DRINKING AS DISTRACTION

A STORY

Every day I feel EXTREMELY lucky to be alive and in the world, on miraculous time. In the spring of 2018 I walked by a Domino's Pizza where in 2010 I passed out drunk and on drugs in the parking lot at, like, six P.M. on a Tuesday and will never forget my friend randomly walking by and waking me up, being like, "Ummmm, hello?"

When I walked by it on that day eight years later, I was like, *DAMN, I LOVE PIZZA*, and also *I can't believe I'm not DEAD and instead I get to live this brilliant life that sometimes is SO INTENSE AND TENDER AND DEVASTATING but mostly MYSTERIOUS and JOYFUL.* Amongst every uncertainty every time you tell me "Good job" or "I love you" or "thank you for your book and your dances and your newsletter," I HEAR YOU, and it's so critical to my aliveness.

Drinking and drugging were my ultimate distractions. I leave us here with a prayer for greater attention.

MAY WE REVALUATE OUR DISTRACTIONS

MAY THEY EITHER BE SPELLS OR WASHED AWAY
MAY EACH DISTRACTION LEAD US TO OUR NEW TRUTH

BOTH THE SMALL ONES AND THE BIG TRUTHS

THE TRUTHS THAT LEAD US BACK TO OUR CENTER

THE TRUTHS THAT HELP US PAUSE
MAY we FORGIVE OURSELVES FOR BEING DISTRACTED,
A SAFETY MECHANISM LEARNED AND INHERITED

MAY we FORGIVE OURSELVES FOR REACHING
PRAYERS FOR NEW WAYS TO REACH

NEW WAYS TO SIT IN IT
NEW WAYS JUST TO BE IN THE RIGHT NOW

CHAPTER 8

Productivity

Part of me just wants to write *HELP ME, HELP ME, please some-one help me learn to be productive!* But I'll tell you what I know about productivity. And what I know about the benefits of throwing it out the window. And then crawling out that window and begging it to come back in. From a very DIY/*I am still learning this* angle. From the perspective of someone who exists within capitalism, just like you! Who believes in working hard but is sometimes so afraid of success and the glow-up that I pretend nothing is real and avoid tasks like it is indeed my job I am clocked into.

I wrote *How to Not Always Be Working* because I couldn't stop working, easy as that. I'm not sure if I was more produc-tive then as much as I was just addicted to working. Addicted to getting things done, attaching my validation as a human to the completion of work.

So I wrote the book, and a backward spell was cast. I started making more money in big chunks all at once. I started being afraid of how big I could be. It made me want to hide, to stay small, to not tell anyone who I was or what I was doing.

It led me to addiction, to not taking care of myself, to never working. It led me to underearning and shame. It led me to being anti-productivity.

Productivity felt uncool. Productivity was for people who were into the four-hour workweek and growing their newsletter lists and getting rich and not paying attention to the sounds of leaves crunching under their feet. Rich people are bad, and productive people don't know how to pay attention to being alive.

These were the stories I grew up being told were true. Success was for celebrities, and those people were probably bad too. Productivity meant I had to accept that I was running a business, that I had to have goals, that I had to work toward something. How could I truly accept the mystery of my aliveness and be productive at the same time? This seemed counterintuitive.

Also—for every one time I tried to be productive, there were three examples of me failing at it. Reaching for the phone, forgetting to make myself meals, losing all effectiveness at what I didn't care about.

I'LL OFFER SOMETHING that has been working for me while I write this book. I've been implementing the Pomodoro Technique—where I write for twenty-five minutes and then take a five-minute break. I do this four times in a row and then I take a fifteen-minute break. While this is a productivity method—I like to think of it as a getting-something-done method. A getting-to-the-thing-I-want-to method.

Because that's the thing about productivity—I want to get to what I want, not let everything slip by my eyes without noticing it. I want this book to be in your hands—hell, I want this book to be in my hands! So having this as a tool for my writing has been monumental.

Another tool for productivity is, basically, the opposite. I think sometimes I need to have HOURS to write. Many, many hours of totally uninterrupted time so that I can let it all flow out of me. But some of my best work comes out of me in fifteen minutes after a walk. Fifteen minutes before bed. These moments add up and become . . . well . . . a book.

They could become your next online class, your next lecture, your next presentation, your next history project, your next podcast episode.

Especially when so much of my life is built around experience, my writing included, I have to remember that LIVING is just important as working. That my rest is essential TO my productivity. Otherwise, what do I have to spring off of? The springboard of work is rest. The springboard of my productivity is a walk where I do absolutely nothing.

So often my guilt around rest, or walking, or care, is that I am not being productive enough. Which brings me to a twofold response to myself. One is that it's good. Being "unproductive" is good. Sitting still and watching a TV show is good. Reading is good. It's all good. Or rather, it's neither good NOR bad. It just is. It's just living. It doesn't have to be named as productive or unproductive. Also, who even invented "unproductive"? You aren't UNDOING ANYTHING. It should just be called "ductive" or "pro" or just "having a damn chill session."

THIS BRINGS ME to the second part, especially for those of us whose lives revolve around creating content for pure creative work and practices. That when you feel your most "unproductive" is when you are gathering your material. You are the researcher. The treasure hunter. The finder of awe and glory. And we need you. We need to know how you see the world. Because we see it so differently from one another, thank god.

I see a sky differently than you see a sky. I sweat differently than you sweat. I hear a leaf crunch differently than you do. And so, in order to know literally anything, we have to be unproductive. The longer we can stay away from productivity, the longer we can gather information to put back into the world as an act of service.

I'm also saying this as someone who avoids. As someone who waits too long. As someone whose unproductiveness easily transforms into distraction, avoidance, and completely falling away from the center I have so carefully attempted to maintain.

This is where the question comes in—is there a line where we can say, *LOOK center! You're so far away! How do I get back to you? And how will I know if I am too far away?*

That is what we are coming back to: How do we know if our pendulum has swung "too far," or is there even such a thing as too far, or is that just invented? This is where we must, we absolutely must, decide for ourselves.

We cannot rely on Buddhist monks or our favorite self-help books or the best productivity blog post to know how to get back to our true center, our place of harmonious activity between rest and work.

One way I check in with this is walking. Another is having a consistent therapist. Another is writing, journaling. And a big one is making an avoidance list.

Having a therapist, a trusted friend, a priest, for God's sake, a sponsor, a mentor, someone who you regularly check in with—is a great way to set your own rules for knowing yourself. Your own rules for knowing when you've gone too far away from your center. With anything, any chapter here—this applies. But something about productivity feels particularly apt. This idea of: *I need to rest, I love to rest!* There are so many amazing resources and books out there that encourage our rest, and twice as many to amp up our productivity.

SO HOW DO we know which end we are on? One activity I love to do is make an avoidance list. And then pick one thing on it to do. Generally this snowballs into a few other things. But I find that a lot of the time when I am feeling distant from a practice of productivity, I can see that it's coming from some level of shame that I've been avoiding things.

I don't necessarily do the thing I want to be productive at, though.

Also, I want to say that productivity isn't bad! Remember on Facebook when you would say you're in a complicated relationship with someone? I'm in a complicated relationship with productivity.

Okay, so back to the list. I look at a few things I have written down.

- ○ Call dentist
- ○ Call mechanic
- ○ Pay IRS bill
- ○ Buy ingredients for chicken salad

I start small. I am avoiding these things. Avoiding these things is increasing my inner shame and guilt. Sure, I could accept that I haven't done these things yet, and just sit with the task at hand and be productive at it. But I have found that one too many times, this is my MO. So usually by the time I attend to one or two things on the AVOIDANCE list, I can get into gear and find myself productive with the thing I want or have to do.

Take writing, for example. Today as I sit to write I feel a much lighter sense of self than I did a few days ago. I had a temp plate on my Jeep and knew I needed to register my license plate. I was late to do it, driving with an expired temp tag. Which, of course, A) made me feel shitty about myself because OF COURSE I have done something like this again! *I can't be an adult*, my inner voice shouts unrelentingly. And B) just the dull blade of shame and guilt for sharing my life on social media, my wins, my triumphs, and the PLEASURE of having a JOB where I get to write books but can't perform this simple adult responsibility, leads me to a dark twisted shame spiral.

Option one: I accept this. I accept I haven't gotten the license plate tag, and I push through and keep writing or working or doing my emails and know I'll get to it when it's time. Some sort of strange acceptance in the avoidance.

But this rots away at my soul. This keeps some little flame inside me burning the candle at both ends. Also, the list is meant to be exciting! Self-esteem boosting! It's meant to be simple.

Last year I heard the phrase "swallow the frog," and it really stuck with me. It stuck with me as a way to tackle the hardest thing first. Because a frog would be disgusting to actually swallow. But it would feel so good to get it over with if you knew it was what you had to do, if you knew when you did it you would feel free and exuberant on the other side. When you wake up, you pick the hardest thing. The thing you have been avoiding the longest. This is your frog. You swallow it whole. You do the task. And because your first action was the hardest one to swallow, every single thing you do following that in the day will feel softer, easier, and less stressful.

I lean into that. I lean into knowing that doing the hardest thing first means all the other things will feel easier.

∘ ∘ ∘

HOW MOTIVATION AND PRODUCTIVITY INTERSECT

I consider my motives and my motivations. What my motives are for: working, not working, exercising, calling someone, texting a crush, opening an app, posting a selfie, buying something, skating?

Maybe the question to ask is: Why do I reach? Why do I avoid? Why do I follow an impulse?

There aren't clear answers, but I offer these to you to just begin a noticing practice, to remember we can choose differently if something isn't working. I've been bringing my phone to bed again, and that means too much phone time in the morning—which usually erases my healthy motivations for work and creativity.

Some days I plan to skate and go to the beach, and I can feel myself wanting to avoid my morning work before I go do those things. My newsletter, emails, working on my book. And when I do that, I don't fully enjoy my leisure and pleasure activities. I want to access great joy, so I commit to sitting and writing first—to stay committed to self and work, even when it's uncomfortable and I want to avoid it.

o   o   o

CYCLES AND SEASONS OF PRODUCTIVITY

This is something I have been really studying for the past few years: my cycles of productivity. These could be within a day, within a month, within a year, within a decade. Really noticing and tracking where my spikes of energy lie, where I need to rest, where I need to crank up the energy, where I need to lean into whatever my true pace is. Paying attention to seasonal productivity levels and needs has been a beautiful and natural way to find my center, to return to myself with ease and patience.

I spent just over one year back in Michigan after a few years in California. I saw all four seasons again for the first time in three years. I was shocked at how comfortable I felt through the winter, how much I grew through the transition into spring, and how much summer lit me up in love and change and creativity.

I spent most of the winter and spring and early summer hosting an artist residency and taking it slow. As summer turned to fall, I found myself in a season of socializing. And as fall set in and started turning to winter, I found myself writing a lot, dreaming about making quilts and carving out more time for art making.

In each season, everything else is sprinkled in. I teach my online class, I write, I dance, I socialize, I update my online shop. But each season is also generally marked more by one specific theme. And as I look back I can start to see where some of the same themes repeat themselves from years prior.

I include this in productivity because, for me, part of learning to be productive is to learn when I am happiest doing something. When it feels the most natural to me. When I don't have to constantly fight myself to put it into place.

FOR THE PAST few years, I have been diligently charting my menstrual cycle. This information may seem relevant to only people who bleed, but sharing this information with all the nonbleeders in my life has really helped them support me and understand what I am going through. When I say, "It's been a hard week four," to one of my best friends, Bobby, he knows exactly what that means and can tap into the kind of support that brings me back to my center.

Every week of a menstrual cycle is different. We have week one, week two, week three, week four, and if you're an unlucky contestant like me, you might also have the mysterious week five, which is just sort of a numb journey of sorrow.

ALAS! As someone who suffers from extreme dysphoria leading up to menstruating, I found that I REALLY had to shift my expectations about what I would be able to do each month of my life. A lot of people who menstruate might find that the days or week leading up to their period are met with waves of depression not comparable to typical PMS symptoms. Week one, I am bleeding, but I am positive—I have ideas and I am also able to rest.

And then we have the powerful week two and three. I have energy, I am excited about life, I am ready to take on the day. My absolute best writing comes out of me, I am channeling spirit, and I love to hang out with friends and I love to think of new projects to do.

And then week four comes, and around day twenty-four I hit a wall. I have had to learn to bring in a lot of extra tools for taking care of myself in week four. Massage, therapy, extra twelve-step meetings, praying. See Chapter 5: Asking for Help.

In this time, I also have to shift my attitudes toward work and productivity. This also is about how we FEEL about our work. I feel like I have the loudest demon in my head during week four. Which is part of what slows my productivity down. Just when I start to think that I am doing an amazing job at something, the inner demon loves to tell me my career is unworthy and going to fail soon and to just quit now.

By paying attention to where I am in my cycle, I can be a little less caught off guard by the evil demon voice and know it's just the week-four voice. Sometimes the inner stories of sabotage creep in any day they goddamn please, but that's a different issue, alas.

Also take note of how the moon cycle affects your creativity. My favorite days to write are a few days after the new moon. A wild thing about the moon is that it literally disappears from the sky. You straight-up just can't see it for a day or two. The night sky is void of all light, all illumination. And this translates into how I feel creatively. I feel the void, I lean into it, and I don't try to fight it. I don't try to fight it because I know what comes next is the waxing crescent, this sliver of light. This promise that the light will return. These are my writing days. These are my fingers-flying-over-the-keyboard days. These are returning-to-center days.

I also want to say returning to our centers or finding them isn't linked to productivity, although I do find it to be an aid in doing so. I do find, though, that once I attain a state of productivity it is usually because some sort of centering practice has worked, and I am closer than I was before.

I am gentle on dark moon days. I take baths, I sauna, I don't push myself too hard, I use compassion with my mind instead of judgment. I greet the day softly, with lower expectations. On full moon days I am awake, I am wide-eyed. If anything I am called to pay greater attention to my personal life and goals. Where does my partnership need shifting? My own patterns of self-care? Does my journaling habit need to come back into my life? I am a little frazzled—everything is illuminated. We see the whole thing.

And then it starts to lessen. We get a little break. We know that what is next is darkness, but we also know that after darkness comes more light.

Pay attention to how the moon plays into your productivity,

creative practice, need for rest, and self-reflection. You will see common themes amongst others, but it is also entirely personal.

The other seasons are daily seasons. This is different for every person, and can also depend on restrictions within your job and its hours. But even adding 1 percent of awareness to these seasons can create major shifts in your day-to-day.

I have noticed that I do my best writing first thing in the day. This does not have a time of day attached to it specifically, it just means first, and it often means actually skipping my morning pages.

This too is up to you to decide how your day looks. Whether it is what happens before and after work, after you put your kid to bed, if it's work-related or pleasure-related or both. Even if you have only one hour of a day, even if you have only ten minutes. It is yours. It is always your time. It is always your body. No matter the shitty job or amazing vacation or perfect thing you're doing or deepest grief you're experiencing—this is your path to and from center, and only you can discover how to prioritize your time and energy.

I see you and I believe in you and how you craft each moment, even the ones you think you're throwing away—they are part of the work too.

o   o   o

A PRAYER FOR BEING LESS PRODUCTIVE

PLAY OUTSIDE
MAKE OUT A TON

DRAW PICTURES OF BIRDS
TURN YOUR PHONE OFF ALL DAY
KEEP YOUR PHONE ON ALL DAY
GO BUY YOUR FAVORITE PENS AT THE ART STORE
COUNT HOW MANY CLOUDS YOU SEE
CLIP YOUR FINGERNAILS
TAKE A BATH
STARE AT THE WALL
DANCE AROUND YOUR HOUSE
DRINK WATER

CHAPTER 9

Validation/Imposter Syndrome

I LOVE YOU ARTISTS

I LOVE YOU WRITERS

I LOVE YOU POTTERS

I LOVE YOU SONGWRITERS

I LOVE YOU CHEFS

I LOVE YOU ACTIVISTS

I LOVE YOU EARTH

I LOVE YOU POETS

I LOVE YOU SINGLE MOMS

I LOVE YOU SHOP OWNERS

I LOVE YOU HERBALISTS

RESIST 45 RESIST PSYCHIC DEATH RESIST BURNOUT

IF YOU'RE AFRAID AND TIRED TODAY, THAT IS NORMAL

THIS IS WHAT THE SYSTEM WANTS

Be willing to pivot, be willing to stay
wildly devoted to yourself

It is my hope and my wish that you ALSO feel infinite gratitude for yourself and for one another in the same way I do—that we can HOLD BOTH is to truly dismantle, to hold the pain and move freely within it. Without you we wouldn't have art and books and movies and poems, and what a THRILL IT IS to witness you making these things and what A GIFT it is for me to be WITNESSED—every single day of my lasting BREATH.

A big part of my imposter syndrome is the idea of leveling up. Of watching my career grow. My success as an artist, a writer. Watching my income grow. Growing, growing, growing. Something we want, we work toward, we strive for.

As a writer, I've often experienced imposter syndrome around not having "well-researched" books or writing. Because I am a dancer, I'm not well-read enough to be a writer. Working in so many different mediums has me sometimes feeling like maybe this would all be easier if I only did one thing. But I've come to believe that each thing informs the others.

Movement is my research, paying attention is my research, morning pages are my research, walking is my research, quilting is my research, listening is my research, and my finished objects are not finished, they are just invitations for more understanding.

o o o

STOP COMPARING YOURSELF.

NOT EVERYONE WILL LIKE WHAT YOU DO—

OTHER PEOPLE WILL REALLY FREAKING LOVE IT.

We attach so much to the acceptance of what we make—art/business/writing/life choices—and that without that acceptance we're worthless, unworthy of love or praise or high self-esteem or self-acceptance. Whether it's longing for the approval of a person, the acceptance of a school or residency you apply to, or simply likes on your feed, we have to take validation out of the equation when we approach our practice of making/being alive.

It's one thing to consider impact; it's another to be paralyzed by fear of what others will think.

I have been known to compare myself to everything and everyone and to hold myself to impossibly high standards. In my writing process I find myself reaching toward self-help books I find incredibly inspiring, but it is quick for me to also deem them better and to immediately decide, *Well, if this book is SO GOOD, what is the point of me writing a book, or doing anything, for that matter?*

I love to watch someone do something, anything—sing a song, sew a quilt, dance a dance, and leave thinking, *THAT made me want to do everything I do better than I've ever done it before.*

But there are other moments when I read things or listen to something that is similar to my own work that makes me go into the demon spiral of, *There is no point for me to ever make anything ever again because enough good things have already been made. THE END.*

This isn't true! A lot of good things have been made, but the things I am making aren't finished being made yet, and I hope never are until the last day I take a breath. So I write. I sit down. I do my best.

In creating ease for myself, I switch the language from *try my best* to *do my best*. I am DOING my best. And my best might not look like anyone else's. My work might not quote a bunch of really famous philosophers or the latest show that was at the Whitney because these are not things I naturally pay close attention to.

I see themes that emerge in other books and think—*Wow, this person is WAY smarter than me I can say to myself*—yes, Marlee, they are. And that's okay. They know a lot more about certain facts and themes and worlds of knowledge than you do, and you know more about the way you inhabit your body, and that's what you are here to write about.

If you feel the doom and gloom around your art, your projects, the people in your life who maybe aren't seeing you or appreciating you the way you want—make a list of what IS working in your life.

Who sees you? Who makes you feel safe? Who loves you unconditionally? Who loves your art? Make a list and keep those people close and remember YOU ARE GOOD.

o   o   o

A PRAYER FOR YOUR IMPOSTER SYNDROME

THERE IS NO ONE LIKE YOU!

YOU ARE THE ONLY ONE WHO CAN DO YOUR JOB!

YOU ARE THE ONLY ONE WHO CAN MAKE YOUR ART!

YOU ARE THE ONLY YOU THERE WILL EVER BE!

YOU ARE HERE FOR A REASON, EVEN IF IT DOESN'T MAKE SENSE!

DOING THINGS THAT OTHER PEOPLE DON'T LIKE DOES NOT MAKE YOU UNCOOL.

DOING THINGS THAT OTHER PEOPLE DON'T LIKE DOES NOT MAKE YOU BAD.

DOING THINGS THAT OTHER PEOPLE DON'T LIKE DOES NOT MAKE YOU UNGRATEFUL.

DOING THINGS THAT OTHER PEOPLE DON'T LIKE DOES NOT MAKE YOU ANYTHING OTHER THAN NOT RIGHT FOR THEM.

YOU ARE GOOD, YOU ARE GOOD, YOU ARE GOOD.

○　○　○

DEFEATING IMPOSTER SYNDROME TOOL KIT

POUR A GLASS OF WATER

LOOK IN THE MIRROR AND SAY SOMETHING LIKE YOU

*ARE HOT AND YOU ARE COOL AND YOU ARE DOING
A GREAT FUCKING JOB!*

*WRITE DOWN THREE PEOPLE WHO AGREE WITH THE
ABOVE STATEMENT*

*CALL THOSE THREE PEOPLE OR TEXT THEM IN THE
NEXT TWENTY-FOUR HOURS. REMIND THEM OF THE
SAME.*

*REMEMBER YOU ONLY HAVE TO LIKE YOURSELF IN
THE FACE OF REJECTION ONE DAY AT A TIME*

MEAN PEOPLE SUCK

WE DON'T HAVE TO BE MEAN TODAY

o o o

NOTES ON WHAT DIFFERENT VOIDS TEACH ME

The new moon phase takes me to places I usually don't know I am ready to go. To places I have so longed for.

In the fall of 2019, I got to spend three days with my peers, my inspirations, and my new and old friends, diving into the depths of our souls with one another and in public at a book festival in Atlanta, Georgia. It was a salve, a balm, one of those warm bags of rice lying on your lower back that says, *You got this, I am here, and we are going to change the world together and be so in love with each other every second of it.*

What I knew moving forward, is we HAVE to be with the people who see us. We HAVE to do our work on the individual level to heal our own ancestral trauma and biases and phobias, to be cracked open. So we can see and listen and hold each other. So we can transform the world into a better future. To be accountable when we fuck up, and grow in our responsibility to our own hearts and our community heartbeat.

I got to that place right on time, we all found one another right on time. Everything is on time keep going!

ECLIPSE SEASONS, WHICH often feel like one long void to me, are whirlwinds, and in moments of celebrating myself I quickly scramble to find ways to make myself small again as quickly as possible. Story lines I like to stay addicted to: I'm not a good friend, I am inconsiderate, I am undeserving of comfort, when I rest I am lazy, suffering is more comfortable and what I deserve, if people don't like me I should just quit everything and become a hermit who never talks to anyone again.

It's getting easier to murder these inner demons that are trying to kill me. These narratives of smallness. There is some truth here, though: the more I step into my joy and my magic and my love and my work, the more it makes people uncomfortable. The good news is those aren't my people. Our people can shift; they have to. It doesn't have to be an earth-shattering shift—it can be an easeful release.

These subtle and sometimes drastic shifts, however, do NOT mean that I am undeserving of love and joy and comfort and rest. In fact, I could be a total shithead today and still make the decision to forgive myself, drink my water and eat my greens (or ice cream for dinner), and still have a few good people who love me unconditionally—and I can choose to join the love-me-unconditionally team a little quicker. Some days, not hating myself is a full-time job, but I'm clocked in, and the other side is really liking myself in the face of personal and career discomfort.

These narratives of self-hatred are distractions from the beautiful and bright world that is around me. Dori Midnight, intuitive counselor and witch, reminds me I am seaweed, wrapped around a sturdy rock, swaying through the water.

PART OF HEALING imposter syndrome and coming back to our center within this work is stepping into this place of not feeling guilty or shy about the way that we are in the world.

I wear a lot of hats (literally, metaphorically). Someone who loves my newsletter might hate my Personal Practice videos. Someone who lives for my IGTV might think my books are trash. People who love the books might hate the online class promotion. People who think I'm a totally great freak in real life might really not know what to do with my internet self.

In the bright light of LOVING DETACHMENT, I absolutely have to let go of what other people think or don't think of me. Usually I am inventing what they think of me or how I think they see me in my head. Am I too loud? Too gay? Not posting enough about being queer? What kind of assumptions are being made about my partnership or my self-worth? Should I share more selfies of me crying? I am sure this would create a great divided amongst followers. PLUS, I have a lot of best friends who I don't follow on social media, and let us all praise the mute button. Mute away. We are not for everyone, or not every part of us is for every person.

Not caring what others think doesn't absolve us from social responsibility to be good people open to critical feedback. I have a lot of work to do! In service to myself, the divine, and YOU! Be gone, distractions from positive self-worth! I am happily stepping into the power of my calling to bring others to the light of art making and self-forgiveness, and to deeply tend to my real-life relationships.

After *How to Not Always Be Working* came out, I got an email from a group of survivors of intimate partner and family violence in Wisconsin who had read it in their book club to remember that their art and self-care practices can keep them safe and alive.

Earlier that same day, I had received an email that my book and my existence were "trash." I had let this feedback really affect me. And THEN seeing the photo of this book club and hearing this, I was like, *WHOA, WAIT, this mean email is not true. It cannot be true because I have been gifted with this other truth.*

We cannot be for everyone, y'all, we simply cannot be, and in the same breath we never know whose life we will change! Please keep making your work and your art, be accountable when called to be, and love yourself in all the ways of being alive.

o o o

MORE ON HOW WE CANNOT FILL THE VOID

I've had to get used to not attaching people not liking what I do to my work. Some people don't like what I do or they don't think it's cool. Whether it's how I live my life or what I write about, or making dance videos on the internet, or literally being a person who uses the internet—there's a myriad of reasons that one might not like what I do.

And maybe I'm lucky that there's been enough of them, that if I were to let that feeling of disapproval impact my work I just wouldn't make anything anymore and I need to make things because 1) I love to, 2) it's my job, 3) it's a service to the world for me to show up in that way. A lot of you seem to resonate with this feeling of thinking, *What are people going to think of this thing when it's done?* and whether that's a choice that you make in your life separate from your work, or it's about an online class that you do, or a zine that you make, or a painting that you paint—whatever it is, I wish that you find comfort in knowing that we all, I think, are running up against that feeling of wanting people to like what we do. And it's really personal. We're living in a world where I think so many of the weird jobs that so many of us have created have a big personal aspect to them, so it's normal to feel that.

But I also wanted to talk about this other side of the coin— when you get what you want. The person that you always hoped would read your book, reads your book. The person that you really wanted that follow-back from, follows you back. You apply to the best artist residency ever, the hardest one to get into, and you get in. You get approved for a loan to make your dreams come true, your crush freaking texts you back— right, these things—this is the good outside validation. But that feeling lasts for me for about twenty-three seconds to a minute and a half until I'm ready for the next one. I'm ready for the next something to make me feel better. I think some of that is being an addict, and someone who deals with codependency. Maybe it's a Gemini thing. A being-alive-during-eclipse-seasons thing. But I wanted to say for myself, and maybe you, that if you get something that you want and A) it makes you feel guilty or B) you lose the high really fast, that's okay and we can recalibrate within that.

So now I know how to lovingly detach from acceptance. I don't need anyone's acceptance. I don't need people to love what I do—I don't need everyone to love it. But then people do start loving it. You do start manifesting what you want. You do get these things. Then you think, *Oh no, I don't deserve this*, or *This is too good*, or *What do I do with all this money?* or *Oh my gosh, this person loves me, what if I fail? Or don't love them back enough*. We can start to spin out.

There's that phrase "In my heart is a god-sized hole"—replace the word "god" with whatever: universe, Spirit of the Universe, ocean.

There's nothing I can actually fill this void with. I can't fill it with likes, I can't fill it with a great career opportunity, I can't fill it with the lavender lemonade from the coffee shop, I can't fill it with cigarettes. I certainly couldn't fill it with alcohol, and I tried my damnedest for so long but the hole is so big that only a spiritual life or a life of generosity or a life of being of service or truly making things for yourself—that's the only thing that's going to fill it. That's a really big hole. So big. I can't even re-create it with my arms.

I'm proud of you for any moment you are detaching from

when people don't like what you make. I also want us to detach from when people do like what we make. Or when we get things that we want. Are we ever enough? Will we ever reach that point of having all the things we want? This might sound a little materialistic, but I'm talking more on a metaphysical plane. Does what we think is going to make us feel better, actually do so? For how long?

The things that I'm putting in my god-sized hole today are sitting still, and drinking water, and making art. Sharing my thoughts with you, and calling friends, and showing up to my practice and liking myself in the chaos of it all. So that's what I've got. I hope you keep making stuff. And keep making really risky big life decisions from right here.

To-Do List for When You're Feeling Unlikable

- Put on a colorful outfit
- Make yourself a cape to wear when you feel like shit
- Call a friend who you know thinks you are the best
- Drink a seltzer and look at your seltzer and say: "We are a team and I like you"
- Take a shower—you might just smell weird and it's making you feel bad
- Stretch
- Go for a walk—nature is super hard to impress cuz she's already so good, she's also not comparing herself to anyone else, which is helpful energy to harness

CHAPTER 10

Grief

Turning now to grief, the part of our soul that experiences deep sorrow and pain at the loss of a life, experience, relationship. The grief that comes simply from an expectation dashed. Sometimes unexpected, sometimes right when we thought it would happen, we can lose ourselves here so quickly.

Grief can be one of the most disorienting feelings that we have. The incomprehensible pain of losing someone or something you love—it whips us into a tailspin where nothing seems possible. We have no sense of self, sense of work, sense of purpose. We can become totally addicted to filling the void with anything in reach: drugs, alcohol, the phone, food, sex, video games, gambling, or turning your partner into your higher power.

This chapter explores how to receive grief with intention, all without abandoning your purpose and practice, your non-negotiable daily commitments, as well as giving yourself full permission to throw it all to the wind in order to let grief move through you.

Part of returning to our center is not avoiding our center. Sometimes the longer we stay there, we have a better chance of not leaving. We have a deeper willingness to stay. We can run from center, we can be knocked off of our center, and we can also choose to dig in and hold on as long as possible.

The holding on is uncomfortable. Escapism is comfortable. We reach, over and over, for anything to take us away from the grief or the joy or any feeling entering our bodies. Partly because we think or assume that this feeling itself is what is going to knock us off our center. *I can't stay with this pain; I'll be ruined. If I feel this heartbreak all the way down, I'll never be able to do anything again. There's no way my body can metabolize these feelings of distress.*

One of the best ways to come back to yourself is indeed to lose yourself completely. To exit all the way. To turn into the crumpled, howling self that came out of the womb. To lose every part of you that is tidy and buttoned and presentable.

As we must stay through discomfort, we must also abandon whatever part of ourselves wants to keep things in.

When ending a romantic partnership, you may feel some of the greatest physical pain you've ever felt, grief that overtakes your whole body. I remember the night John told me he wasn't in love with me anymore. When he left, I laid on my giant circular rag rug and wailed and cried harder than I ever had. I felt like an animal wounded in the forest.

I didn't want to feel that pain. In the past I would have immediately drunk over it, smoked, done drugs, anything to numb myself from knowing that what I wanted wouldn't be there anymore. But my body overtook those feelings and did its thing. It passed through my body and into the ether and, even while still in great pain, I was able to carry on with my life.

This is a small moment; this wasn't a death of a person, but it was the death of an ideal. And sometimes people staying alive is just as much an attachment to an idea—the idea that they will continue to be alive without us, mourning the loss of someone living.

We all die. Everything dies. Accepting this, basking in this, brings us to ourselves again and again when we are taken away.

We must rest; we must lean into whatever is happening. Grief takes time. It is not linear. Neither is joy, or time, or love. We wish and we worry and we pray, but only the will of the universe is in order, and it is in perfect order whether we believe it or not.

This is often the hardest part of grief: our lack of acceptance. Of course there is denial and anger that we often feel first, and then comes sadness and loneliness, an inability to comprehend that what we have lost will never be ours again.

Releasing our expectations around grief is one of the best ways to not get surprised by it. I find that in partnerships and friendships with folks who have a parent who has passed on, grief can come in in sneaky ways. They fall in love with a new person and realize that that parent will never meet their partner, never meet their new dog, see their accomplishments, be at their wedding, text them.

We meet this two ways—we let it suck. This is also a way to support someone who is experiencing this: remind them it is okay, that it completely and totally sucks, and that getting caught off guard by grief is normal.

We want to wrap it in a bow. Yep! Dealt with that super-sad and tragic life event. But deep within the unknown mystery of life, there are always more surprises. Always more ways that it will come up. While this is often an act of survival, to paint the beautiful picture too soon, it can also prevent us from facing our feelings completely. To assume that a grief pattern is finished could be really helpful to you, but it's also good to remember that it can sneak back in. And when it does, it simply has more to teach us, and we can let it be a gentle lesson.

HOW THE HELL do we do this? When everything falls apart, I return to my daily habits. And in these heightened states of being, I tend to forget them again and again. The year I went through my divorce was documented on my Personal Practice Instagram account, where I filmed myself dancing every single day for the full year. A lot of days I didn't want to. I just wanted to be sad and not show anyone. But for me it was this amazing experience of still fully showing up for my commitment, despite how much pain I was in. More often than not, filming myself dancing helped move something inside of me, something I hadn't been able to name yet—but when dancing meets grief, it leads me to this deep knowing of myself.

It is also about returning gently to the self. If you have a practice that is set up to serve you but that grief has taken you out of, be gentle with yourself as you get back to it. Return to center with care and with compassion for the self. Beating the shit out of yourself to get back to yourself—it's really just mean. It's not kind. It's obnoxious, and it's a disservice to the collective. We need you! We need you to be kind to yourself, even when you've really fucked up or failed or want to quit everything.

You can still assume you are the worst person and be really nice to yourself. I promise, I do it many days in a row sometimes. Make a list of your nonnegotiable daily commitments. Try them, rearrange them constantly. Forgive yourself every two minutes when you do not do them.

This is what we call building complete and utter relentless faith in the universe.

Yes, it took until chapter ten, but I am here now to tell you the universe has a divine and specific plan for you. And it's so magnificent. But we only get to have it if we pay very close attention. Here are suggestions for how to do so.

o o o

WAYS TO STAY WITH THE FEELINGS OF GRIEF, QUESTIONS FOR CONSIDERATION

Roll your neck around. It's sort of like taking a deep breath but in movement. I find that stillness can be so uncomfortable when I am teaching myself how to feel my feelings. It may become clear now that my reoccurring neck injury comes from holding feelings there. I don't let them flow from my brain to my heart. The throat and neck seem like the most direct physical pathway. This assessment is not scientific but intuitive.

What are sadness and grief when it is your expectations that aren't being met? When you want something from someone and they can't give it to you?

What is sadness when someone else's highest good makes you sad?

What is sadness when you feel alone but you aren't actually alone?

What fears come up when you think you can't do something by yourself?

What are you afraid of around will and hope and wonder?

When someone else makes a choice that is for their highest good, how do you reconcile when it isn't in line with what you wanted or hoped for?

How do you stay true with your words in your reaction time?

○ ○ ○

WHEN I HAVE an outcome in mind or a commitment is made to me and then that shifts for someone, how do I support them in staying true to their path, while acknowledging and accepting that it has put me off course?

HOW DO I know what my course is?

More often than not, the course that is laid out for me, the course that is offered to me, is one of great bountiful fruits. It is one that I can't even see on my own yet. It is one that has meaning and depth to me, but I can't see it. This is also where grief meets the unknown. I grieve when I think I have known something, but it turned out not to be true. It isn't that it isn't true, it's simply not the way I wanted it. Sometimes this feels bratty or I feel little Marlee bubble up in an unexpected way. She wants her teammate, she wants to be supported, she wants to be held and to be close. But adult Marlee is driving the car, and she has the ability to run the course true to self.

It's the expectations of others also. If a partner or friend makes a commitment that affects the expectations of other loved ones—how do we reconcile that? This is a long list of questions, not because I don't know the answer, but because I have to continuously ask myself these questions. Getting to center is a spiral. It is a circle. It is continuous and it is long and it will go on and on until our last breath.

This is both overwhelming to me and creates peace. It creates a serenity knowing that my days will be a series of reminders and rememberings. A series of thinking I know and then realizing I know nothing. A series of almosts and what-would-have-beens and *What if I'd done this?* and *What could I have done differently?* But that's the thing about what-ifs—it doesn't matter, because they are not reality. What-ifs are a series of defying god, defying what is true and what is known. And what is known is nothingness. Groundlessness. Complete abandon to the process.

So we are allowed to grieve. We attach grief to the big stuff—death of a parent, a partner, a child. Ending of a job, losing a house, losing a friendship. What is common about big grief and little grief is that it is all just grief—not having something you thought you would have. Not having something you loved having. Not having something you thought would also be close to you. A person, an idea, a relationship, a project.

This is the grief that sneaks up, that sneaks in. Quiet as a mouse, rummaging its way through the cheese of your heart. You know it's there, and you can sort of hear it, but you think,

This shouldn't be here! I laid the mousetraps and I cleaned the fridge and I swept the crumbs, so this mouse CANNOT really be here. But it is, and we have to deal with it. No, not deal with it. We have to invite it over for a three-course meal and see what it has to say.

When we deny ourselves the little grief, we get sick. We get small. We hurt ourselves and we hurt those around us by projecting onto them what is unprocessed within ourselves. There is no guidebook that says this is a big enough loss for you to feel grief. And when we measure our grief next to someone else's, we are sure to block it from our bodies.

It's also allowed to just suck. The small grief. Your partner can't get work off to do something they promised you they would do. A friend has to cancel a walk in the woods. Your soft-boiled egg at seven minutes looked like a ten-minute hard boil for some unknown reason, and you just can't fucking grapple with how this could have ever happened.

You feel off course, and it's allowed to suck.

You feel alone, and that's allowed to suck.

But let's pull back the layers together. That's part of finding our centers too—there are so many centers. There is the center within you, the center of the Earth, the center of your past present and future partners. The center of your hands and the center of your solar plexus. There are so many layers that surround each of these centers it's no wonder the layers are thick and they make us cry like a damn onion when we peel them back. This is the work. To peel and peel and peel, over and over again, to see what's there.

During the center residency, herbalist/designer/friend Jade

Marks reminded me that anger is often a mask or a shield for grief. That it is blocking the sadness about something totally different that actually has nothing to do with the situation at hand.

When I am disoriented and angry, there is almost always grief underneath that. Grief and fear. I am afraid to do something alone, I am afraid I won't be loved, I am afraid that this one shift or pivot by someone is a reflection on my own enoughness.

When I'm in this state of mind, I give myself two choices—I can act out of fear or I can act out of love and compassion. To the self and to others. When I act out of fear, it delays the process of getting to center and puts me further off course.

These are places you can go to; you can peel back the layers to see what is there. Because here is the thing—we are strong and we can do that. We are able to do the big, big stuff. If you are here—reading or listening to these words—you are ready to do the scary work of being alive.

And that is enough! The willingness to be willing is enough to begin. To begin before you're ready. To begin in the mess of it all—that is enough.

CHAPTER 11

Joy

Joy will always leave; it will always be fleeting. So when we find it, when we fully and unabashedly tap into it—we must keep it close, keep it holy.

This is an experience we don't want to miss: being alive and being joyful. Guilt around joy stems from this feeling of *why me?* Why should I get to feel joy when so many people in the world cannot access it?

This is the thing about crossing the river, crossing the stream. When we experience joy and let it fuel our lives and our journey to the other side, we can share this with others close to us, privately and publicly, to show them that it is also possible to feel this feeling.

This doesn't mean we can't fall sometimes ourselves. I often attach the word "deserving" to my level of joy. Do I really deserve this life of joy and abundance? Part of learning to accept my joy is being generous with it, being the portal that shows those who are two steps behind in my current life lesson how I got to the other side.

If we don't do this, we all drown, and no one wants that. Or, if people want that for you, they are not your people and have a different river they can get in. Last time I checked there are a shit-ton of rivers in the world, so remember, if someone doesn't want to get in your boat or there is a boat of joy or lived experience you don't want to get in, that's okay.

I DON'T WORRY too much about longevity or the sustainability of projects. Which, I suppose, from a business strategy or how-to-make-a-partnership-last perspective, would be terrible advice. But what even is "ADVICE," YA KNOW?! It's worked great for me to just, one day at a time, look around and see what I want to pay attention to, and go with that. If I am not tending to my divine self, how the fuck will I show up for everyone else? AND THIS is how I want to integrate joy into my whole world.

The pendulum swings, though, and joy and exuberance and pleasure can engulf us—knocking us off our centers just as quickly as grief or inner pain.

Joy mixed with addictive qualities around a new relationship, the excitement around an idea or shift, joy around something finally being over, can cause a hazy glow over what might be better suited to be considered mundane.

When I start to feel feelings for a new person romantically, joy overtakes me. And more often than not, this joy shifts into complete and total fantasy. *I've finally found "the one." I will never feel sad again! This person is going to complete me.* All of my focus and energy goes into obsession; my thoughts are not my own. They are from some part of me buried within that hopes that something external can really "fix" me. That whatever is "wrong" with me will finally be healed by this one THING. This one person, this geographical move, this new object I will buy.

Sometimes this turns out to be true. A new love does enter and provides a prosperous healthy partnership that fills me with nourishment. I move to a new place and my self-care and work ethic strengthen. I purchase something that enhances the way I care for myself and others. But it's hard for me to let it be just that, and not think that the thing itself will indeed be the thing that finally changes me.

I stay addicted to joy, but then I also try to get rid of it because I feel guilty. My sobriety plays into this narrative too. I've been witness to friends dying, suicides, accidental overdoses, relapses, lives of suffering due to drugs and alcohol. So why did I get to stay? Why do I get to have a life beyond my wildest dreams?

I don't know the answer, but I know to shift into gratitude for that. And that lives lost are never lives wasted. No death is in vain. So many of the faces I think of who aren't here anymore proved to me in their waking days and in their off-Earth days that life is magic, and we have to keep trying, and they didn't fail— their course just didn't include being on this realm anymore.

And so we stay joyful for them. And we stay joyful for ourselves, and we stay joyful for whoever wants to get to the other side of the river. I almost said whoever "needs" to get to the other side of the river, but generally those people aren't always who seek help or guidance. We have to want this; we have to want to return to our center. To get to the other side. Needing it is one thing, but wanting it is another.

Being in service to joy also means not fully swinging on the pendulum I spoke of earlier. It means staying on the beam, staying in the center. Because slipping into obsession can cause so much disorientation you won't remember how you got there in the first place.

Here are some ways I notice and pivot in this space, when joy turns to fantasy and *fix me* thinking.

- A relationship is in the first week, and I'm certain they are perfect and we will never break up and all my prayers have come true
- I start to feel "not good enough" when my partner isn't paying constant attention to me
- My partner's mood or acceptance of me is how I navigate my own mood
- I stop doing the things that make me feel happy and joyful on my own
- I worry about what other people think of my actions and value
- I assign myself worth to having a partner/my partner, to other people's acceptance of me

THIS IS NORMAL. They don't call it the honeymoon phase for nothing. Or wanting to be liked—this is normal. They call it that because no matter where you are, it really does feel like you are on a beach on a tropical island, and you aren't sweating, you're glowing, and nothing can touch you.

Here's the thing, though: something can touch you, and it's called reality.

So when you're in this space, greet it! Say hello to it. Notice it. Find out what is underneath the fantasy. What are you afraid of? What do you want to avoid feeling?

My two answers are generally: heartache and autonomy. I don't want to face the fact that something could not work out, specifically be out of my control. And I also don't want to face that I might be alone again in a forced state of autonomy. Which of course is a strange fear since when I am fully autonomous—partnered or not—I am my best self. What I am getting at here is it is scary for me to be my best self.

FROM THE FALL of 2018 to the summer of 2019, when I was single for eight months with one romantic tryst in the midst of it, that one romantic moment spun me out for longer than I'd care to admit.

Let's break that down—"Longer than I'd care to admit." She was magical, she was shiny, like a unicorn person that you know is probably going to destroy you. But the way she's talking to you, you're sure it's magic, and we can trust magic, so there's nothing to worry about.

Alas, I hung on to an IDEA of what I wanted it to be, an idea of what it could have been. So many other relationships at least get to play out, you see if they work or don't work. While there was time spent together in real life, our phones were the tether for our feelings, and the phones were microphones for what we wanted to see happen but couldn't make into a reality.

I drove seventeen hours through a dangerous blizzard to see her once because I thought that was a very good idea. Is it wild, romantic love?! *I'm just adventurous*, I thought to myself!

Plus, what if I NEVER LOVE AGAIN? I thought as I approached the final hour of the drive to a person who I really hardly knew in the first place.

But the joy of a new relationship drove me (quite literally) to act without abandon and throw me off all the other commitments I'd made or things I had planned on working on.

It was something to obsess over. It was something I chose to knock me off my center.

o　o　o

THE OKAYNESS OF FLEETING JOY

Many days I can access joy, but sometimes only for a few hours or even moments. For example, once, in a three-hour state of joy, I remembered that this WILL ALSO PASS, and this is not sad. It is to be celebrated, just as we apply the saying THIS TOO SHALL PASS to all the sad hard days, the good days will also pass. Right on by. Back to the big sad, the discomfort.

This realization also reminded me that I always reemerge—even if just for a moment. It wasn't to put a damper on my joy, but to just look it in the face and say, *Yes: I see you, you have returned! I know you will leave me again, but if I study you and pay sweet attention, I'll know it's you again when you inevitably return.*

o　o　o

JOY AVOIDANCE

I often say, "I don't have writer's block, I have a SITTING-DOWN-to-write block." But I love to write. It's my second-favorite thing to do, right after teaching dance class. Which is another thing I do less than ten times a year. So take note of this pattern—find it within yourself.

When I sit down to write, with my damn snacks and my spicy water, my ambient music blasting, spirit flows through me and the words get written. I love to write. I love that writing for myself and for you is my job. What a sweet gift I've received. But wanting to stay small haunts me every day! EVERY SINGLE DAY, I fight the part of me that wants to avoid my joy and my magic and my curiosity, and I want to stay in the numbness of addiction and self-sabotage.

This is where we turn gratitude into an action. While writing a gratitude list and expressing gratitude is helpful, putting it into action helps me maintain self-respect—which in turn leads me into the joy of the action itself. If I want to be grateful, I have to treat my objects, tasks, and responsibility with great respect.

o   o   o

I SAY THIS little prayer:

TODAY I WILL NOT FIGHT

I invite this inner demon to sit with me while I write.
HELLO little demon, you cannot fuck with me today
but you may sit next to me while I sip my beverage

*and eat my seaweed snack. Thank you for wanting me
to be THE BEST but I have work to do. Even if it's B+
mediocre work, it's my excellent work and it's time.
LET'S GO.*

*Publicly sharing joy can feel vulnerable, more so for me
than sharing my deep struggles, so when I am tapped
into limitless joy I try to really stay with it. Lean into it.*

o o o

TAKING CARE OF WHERE YOU LIVE OFFLINE AS A JOY ACCESS POINT

One thing that is important to me about joy is finding out where my neighbors find joy. At the library, bingo night, the coffee shop. There is an event in Detroit called Hareoke that is the most joyful event I know of. It's hosted by Cole Davis, and they bring their entire wig collection, props, and more—they dress each person up to feel like their best and most beautiful self. And then we sing songs to one another and laugh and dance and eat pizza. This is where my community goes for joy.

I notice which restaurants feel joyful, both in the staff and the patrons; which walking trails have the happiest dogs; which beaches have the widest range of bodies expressing joy. I go toward joyful spaces, because more often than not, if I am not finding it, I just need to do a little more research to locate where it is outside the confines of my own home/my own mind. If you aren't finding joy in your normal patterns, switch up your routine and continue looking around you. Michigan's state motto is

"If you seek a pleasant peninsula, look about you." How sweet! Look about you—apply this to your joy practice.

o   o   o

FINDING JOY BY STAYING CURIOUS IN THE PROCESS OF SELF-REFLECTION

I want to talk about self-inquiry, self-reflection, and how to practice them without hating ourselves—in fact, how to do them while letting this endless joy fill ourselves up to take us to the highest places of good.

There are so many different tools, different teachers, different ways that I take an inventory of myself. Whether that's in therapy, twelve-step rooms, or taking written inventories, reading different books from different teachers, following accounts on social media—whatever it is—I'm constantly in this state of self-reflection, and that can get really tiring. I was asked in an interview once, "Do you identify as a self-help author? Or does that put you in a box?" And I thought, *Well, I am an author, I am a writer, and I write about helping myself, so I guess that's what it is.*

It started bringing up things about what my responsibility is to myself or to the world when I'm in this place of constant self-reflection.

Whether it is your job or not, whether you're a writer or a therapist or a coach or a guide or a healer in this world, I feel like most people who are reading this, or who I am in conversation with, are also in this portal of deep self-reflection.

When my physical pain comes, it's easy to think, *WOW, it'd be SUPER COOL, Marlee's Body, if you could just NOT do this* instead of thinking, *Wow, interesting, body. What are we working through, what are we working on today?* When I have any sort of flare-up, with my physical health, relationships, mental health, I can feel like, *Is anything right? Is anything working?* instead of asking, *What's right? What's working? What's bringing me joy?*

It's a very subtle shift in curiosity that brings me into joy and into gratitude.

Sometimes it seems like my generation has been called in to look at the hard stuff, to break these family patterns, this ancestral trauma. We are looking at things both in our tangible, physical bodies that are here now and in what has been inherited and passed down to us.

This also means we HAVE to let joy in. We have to let it in or this deep inner reflection is going to wear us down in ways that will not be sustainable.

I'm sending the gift of curiosity and joy and lightness to our self-reflection, which I think is so necessary. If you're looking at that really, really hard stuff, stay curious, keep it interesting. What's in there? What's going on in there? How can I go all the way in and look so closely, but know that the gift I will give myself on the other side is the radical acceptance of joy in my life?

And when I do experience joy, I will practice not running from it. I will stay curious to how it came up, curious as to why I want to run from it, and I will stay in healthy conversation with this joy. And remember that when I feel joy, it ripples out to others—oftentimes others who need it more than me.

CHAPTER 12

Vulnerability

In the public sphere, vulnerability comes easy to me. Or perceived vulnerability and braveness. More often than not, people thank me or reach out to me in gratitude for the way I so publicly share my life.

But the barometers of vulnerability are different for everyone. For me, bringing my car to the mechanic and admitting I have no idea what's going on is vulnerable.

Sitting with my partner and looking her in the eyes and telling her my fears is vulnerable.

Grocery shopping and not knowing what exactly goes together and feeling like I don't know how to assemble a damn meal is vulnerable.

Don't get me wrong: sometimes when I share certain things publicly it is extremely vulnerable, but I would say probably only 10 percent of the time. The other 90 percent, I am performing; I am taking what I have researched and my lived experience and synthesizing into a presentation for public consumption.

Now, before you decide that I've been faking vulnerability, let me assure you, the behind-the-scenes labor is where the vulnerability lies. The output has been part of my life's work since I was five years old and first realized I loved to jump on the couch and do a dance and have everyone watch. The witnesses were joyful, happy. So for twenty-seven years I've been living that way, to see how when I take my own joy and pain and wonder and awe and swirl it into words and movement—it is how I know how to be in my body and in my life.

But the vulnerable parts are what you don't see, are sometimes what I don't show anyone.

For some of you, sharing publicly may be EXTREMELY vulnerable. Terrifying. The last thing you'd ever want to do. There are a few parts to this:

A. That's okay. It might mean you are not ready. You may need more time to understand your own experience or another's. You might not be fully ready to say out loud what is boiling inside of you. If this is the case, we don't need to attach a single ounce of shame or guilt to this. It is your pace, and you get to decide your pace.

B. You're afraid you're not good enough—this one just isn't true. Moving on.

C. You're afraid you'll say something wrong.
   a. If you're speaking on your own experience in the

world, you can't really say something wrong. It's YOUR process and it's YOUR experience as a human you are sharing.

a. If you're speaking on a topic that is new to your understanding or you simply don't know enough about it yet, pause and do the research, especially if you hold privilege in the topic you want to speak out on. Find teachers and pay for them for their knowledge; go to the local library and find books on the topic. Find the harmony between the urgency of the world needing your voice, and the patience it might take you to catch up.

IN FARIHA RÓISÍN'S book of poetry, *How to Cure a Ghost*, on page twenty-six you'll find these words:

you are here for a purpose!
you are here for a purpose!
you are here for a purpose!
you are here for a purpose!

In perfectly pink ink, you receive this reminder, and knowing that part of our purpose IS vulnerability. Fariha offers us this act of service that is funny yet difficult to swallow, and carries a feeling of easeful togetherness throughout—as if she's just talking directly at you—no filter, nothing to hide.

When we do this, we heal a part of ourselves. We also offer the gift to someone else who doesn't have words yet for their own vulnerability.

WE NEED EACH OTHER! WE NEED BOOKS! How else will we ever find ourselves? Blessings abound to everyone putting their tender hearts on the page for all of us to see—books teach us about the human condition; writing about this is one of the most vulnerable acts.

AS I'VE MENTIONED before, I have a tendency complete and total asshole TO MYSELF. Let me zoom in on this a bit.

Not moderately unkind. Not sort of hard on myself. Not a little bit mean sometimes. A TRUE DERANGED MONSTER OF A PERSON trapped inside my mind wants to kill me every day. And I don't say "kill" lightly. Wants to lead me to the cliff, to the bottle of tequila, to the END.

I find it getting worse and louder as I step into my bigness! Or, hell, it's probably not even that big. I'm just stepping into myself. I had a big life season in May–July 2019 where my work started feeling really good, I taught an amazing dance work-shop, I was flowing writing this book, my online class was a blast, I fell in freaking love with Jackie, the residency was more beautiful than ever, I tackled my debts and money shame, and then BOOM—a sneaking voice said, *YOU CAN'T HAVE ALL OF THIS. THIS IS NOT FOR YOU.*

Sometimes I let the voice win. I let it sabotage me back into smallness. Into underearning, impulse spending, not trusting my relationships, and just generally being really mean to my-self.

SO, WE WORK TIRELESSLY TO CHANGE THIS. AND BY "WE," I MEAN ME AND WHATEVER DEMON VERSION OF MARLEE IS

TRAPPED IN MY BRAIN AND SPINE THAT HURTS. And by "we," I maybe also mean you and me because maybe YOU GET IT or maybe you murdered this voice long ago. I SURE FUCKING HOPE YOU DID.

It's just practice. I just have to practice being nice to Marlee today. One day at a time. Because she's pretty awesome and cool. I just forget. Or, after keeping myself low for so long—it's more comfortable to be there. Quitting drinking nine years ago was hard because being numb and blacked out WAS SO COMFORTABLE. But now being sober is so comfortable. I make lists of THINGS TO DO to not be an asshole to myself, but I think that's part of the problem—I can't act my way out of it. I have to change this one from the inside. I want to get INVESTIGA-TIVE—OH! I hate myself right now! I wonder why that is. Maybe I'll try a different feeling toward myself now.

o   o   o

A PRAYER AND A PLEDGE FOR VULNERABILITY

I pledge to be willing to grow, to earn, to be in love, to love, to see, to notice. And I pledge that when I forget to do these things, I will not be an asshole to myself. I will be nice to myself and I will just DO IT: I WILL JUST BE NICE and hopefully this practice will bear endless gifts for us all.

o   o   o

AND THIS, THIS searching, has been one of my most vulnerable states. Not sharing it out loud or in writing form—by the time I am ready to share it I don't feel the vulnerability factor as much.

But going through the muck is where I am most vulnerable. When the wound is fresh, when I don't want to look myself in the eye because I have to clean up the mess. Or arrange the mess. Put it on the shelf, tidy it up, make sense of it all, Marie Kondo my damn life.

o o o

VULNERABILITY AND IDENTITY

A big part of getting to center for me has been coming face-to-face with my sexuality, the parts of me that were hiding, and accepting the journey it took me to get there.

I assumed that being "in the closet" meant that you had to be miserable and hate having sex with whoever you were dating or married to and that you knew you were in the closet. I think that's a common myth that people even know they are in the closet to begin with. It wasn't until I started dating women that I began to unravel everything that had happened in my past that I had ignored, pushed deep inside me, pushed back into the closet of my awareness.

I found a poem I wrote when I was fifteen years old where I talked about a girl I had a crush on in detail, but there had been "accusations" that I was the "ballet lesbian," and in the poem I made sure to say that I was NOT a dyke.

Sixteen years later I am glad to report to you that I am indeed a dyke and the accusations were true, but until I found this poem buried in a box of notes at thirty-one years old, I honestly hadn't remembered that happening. And then all of a sudden it came flooding back.

Growing up in a world of ballerinas generally consists of two kinds of people: straight women and gay men. Now, of course there are straight men and queer women ballerinas, but in general that's who is visible in the ballet world. Thankfully this is changing and always evolving, with more and more queer and varied bodies showing up in dance and ballet.

Reading back over how I felt in what is one of the cheesiest and sincere poems I have ever read brought me back to this pain, which I had completely pushed away. I was vulnerable and then I was made fun of. I was called a lesbian and a dyke, and I was made to feel in this pivotal moment that those were gross and bad things to be, and so for the fourteen years that followed, I made sure to never be those things.

At some point in my early twenties it became clear I was queer and was surrounded by a queer community that supported and elevated this feeling and made me feel safe. I still, however, could not link my sexual desire for women to my love for women. I felt both, but I kept them separate. I didn't remember what happened in high school, but my body remembered and my subconscious remembered, and god forbid I wouldn't be accepted again.

When my now ex-girlfriend and I started dating, so many memories came flooding in every time I felt the truth of my sexuality and just pushed it away. I think words can be loaded and scary, and I remember vehemently being like, "Well, I'm not a LESBIAN." I held on to it as this dirty word, a curse. The curse of being the ballet lesbian was something I never wanted to feel. And for someone who was approaching thirty, the vulnerability of having to start over seemed impossible to me. I felt like a fraud. *Can I really be gay? I married a man, after all, and I loved him and had a good sex life! Maybe I'm just still queer or bisexual.* And of course sexuality is fluid, ever changing, and for many people this could have been true.

Part of other people's online vulnerability is what saved me, what brought me into myself, and why I never want to shame any of our use of the digital sphere in this way. I started following accounts and reading the books they suggested, I read every Audre Lorde poem I could get my hands on, I read *Our Right to Love: A Lesbian Resource Book* from front to back. I cried and cried and cried and saw myself for what felt like the first time ever.

I can't help but look back and think: What if my vulnerability had been protected? What if I had felt safe enough to fight back or stand up for myself in these moments of confusion? What if I had had more examples of women loving women in my life?

When someone comes to you with their vulnerability, they trust you. We have to hold each other through that. Sometimes vulnerability first shows up as anger. When I am angry, I often pause to ask myself, *What is really under there? What are you too afraid to share?* And to also start a sentence off with "This is really vulnerable for me to share" is a signal to my partner or to loved ones that I am in a sensitive space and am seeking a tender listener. It also gives the listener a chance to say if they are available emotionally for the labor of being the listener, and if not, maybe I can find someone else to be the listener.

I pray that your vulnerability is kept safe, that you find people who see and celebrate you for exactly who you are. That whenever you start to see yourself, you know that you are right on time. There is no wrong time to emerge. To begin your vulnerable journey back to your center. Someone else has probably walked the pathway before—follow their steps, make your own. Only you can carve out this sacred space for yourself.

CHAPTER 13

On Discomfort

When I consider something like "my stamina for life," I think a lot about survival. Not just self-care, but really making it through the day. Because there are so many different kinds of days, ones filled with ultimate and exuberant joy, and ones where trauma and pain and hardship and grief do their best to tie us down.

We look inward—which is where the stamina begins. An inward reflection toward self—and asking, *What is the next right thing? What is the next right thing I can do to get me to the next right thing after that?* These are tools I build in to sit with the discomforts of life.

Filling a glass of water seems to be a common theme for me—if I have no idea what to do next, what to do to get me out of whatever brain spin cycle I am in, filling a glass of water is usually a good first step. Jamila Reddy, friend and coach and what I would consider an expert on joy and grief, reminds me often of the importance of hydration. "Don't be dry," they say.

I carry this with me often. Then comes the next step, which is usually pen and paper. What do I actually need to do next today? Maybe I even just write the word "NOTHING" on a piece of paper.

Productivity, what is it? Why do we want it? Because "capitalism" is maybe too easy to say. Maybe too brief, too simple. But it is because of living under capitalism that we think we should always be productive. Even in my headspace while writing *How to Not Always Be Working*, or writing parts of this book, I can find myself in this space of wanting to excavate all of these parts of myself in hopes of being more productive.

What if we were still just because being still is important? I often get confused and consider my morning pages to be a practice place for me as a writer. Or think that the ritual of doing it every single day will make me better at my job or my work. This is not inherently why I do morning pages, though. I do them because they give me stamina for my life. I do them because I love to practice. To practice just to practice is the most important thing to me.

If morning pages are just for practicing, and eating is just for eating (not to fuel you through your day like a productivity monster), I think we will start to see our stamina in a new way.

I'll never forget when I told my dad, "When I stay hydrated and drink a lot of water, I can work so much better!" And he responded, "You also just have to drink water to stay alive." In that moment, I could really see where I had attached productivity to every single thing I do, even the task of staying alive. Staying hydrated. I reached for my water just as I typed that and remembered another thing that has become important to me—a revelation I had after *How to Not Always Be Working* came out: any given action can be both/and.

When I reach for the water, and I drink it, it can just be drinking water. In that moment, I do it for no other reason than to let water enter my body. I look out the window. I am taking a pause from this writing. I am hydrating. I write better when I am hydrated.

It can really be both/and. Another stamina for life builder. In the fall of 2018, I took a stint at surfing. It became my favorite thing. I never really stood all the way up on the board, but just paddling out and riding waves on my knees and sitting and staring at the moon became a practice for me. And it felt good how incredibly disconnected from my work it was. It added to swimming, the activity I always think of as the way I cracked the code to not always working.

But then my newsletter became a damn surfing diary. And I got so mad at myself. Can I keep anything out of my work? NO! And this isn't bad—as long as the task at hand, the task of practicing and showing up and being in the moment, stays exactly that. I am allowed to bring my life experience into my writing—in fact, that is indeed my work.

Staying hydrated, swimming, surfing, skateboarding, practicing, morning pages, writing just to write. Dancing just to dance. Even if it's documented, shared, processed. Keep them holy while they are happening. Stamina builders. I also feel a certain kind of comfort in the tiredness. If I had to choose one—the severe coffee buzz with a stomachache and my head feeling weird OR this tiredness but with a body clarity—I choose tired, body clarity!

o   o   o

EXERCISE: BREATHING IN THE COLLECTIVE

Pema Chödrön's gift is Bodhicitta—an exercise of breathing in the collective feeling for everyone who feels it, and on the exhale breathing out relief for all of us.

When you are in the deepest discomfort—let's say you're feeling extremely lonely—take a deep breath in for every single person who feels loneliness. And then when you breathe out, breathe out relief for everyone feeling this feeling. This simple exercise not only lets us move toward a feeling instead of running away from it, it's also a way to energetically tap into healing for all. And a reminder that you are not the only one in discomfort.

That is so often the most isolating feeling—thinking that we are the only ones who feel a feeling. That no one else understands our pain or must be feeling better than we are. Creative practice is also how we can fill the void in a new way. Creative practice heals us. Making things is what we can reach for. Making things is how we process being alive.

o   o   o

Tools

- Journaling and quiet time as a way to process
- A grief support group
- Making a zine about your grief and discomfort

- Making a zine about your joy
- Embrace intimate storytelling in your chosen medium: painting, drawing, singing, dancing
- Channel it into your creative practice
- A walk
- Writing a letter
- Deep breathing
- Stretching
- Swimming
- Prayer and meditation

o   o   o

AND THEN THE GUILT so many of us feel when we encounter the joy or relief that can come from working through discomfort. Giving permission: we must continue to remember that feeling joy is our divine right and purpose—it is why we are here. The amount of suffering in the world is beyond what we can even see.

Building awareness as fuel for empathy: Reading the news, being aware of what is happening in your neighborhood, community, and world is so important. Ignoring it does not protect us from our own joy. It can simply help us see what is happening to other humans. Even when it is uncomfortable. And then let that push us into doing more and more joyful work—so that we can access empathy and collective grief, and create work that inspires.

There is this fear: *What if I was really my best self? Would I still be respected?* So much of my self-acceptance came from struggling. A friend once said to me, "It feels like a betrayal to the struggle to leave the struggle." And it does, it still does.

But what if I had kept getting drunk every day just because I didn't want to leave my alcoholic friends behind? I'd be dead. I'd be six feet under. And today I get to watch stepping into that light inspire many others to put their own addictions down or face them in new and honest ways. Stepping into your light and magic is important and necessary FOR the struggle. The world and the people in it need us—so if you are standing on a precipice of accessing joy and stepping away from discomfort, by all means take the leap!

Today I want to manifest stepping into joy unapologetically. This is not a place I easily step into. I felt guilty every time I did something that brought me joy. Feeling like I didn't deserve it. I hadn't suffered enough or had too much privilege to feel it.

I am inspired when I surround myself with others who step into their joy and share that process with the world. This gives me permission to do the same. Leaving the struggle is in no way a betrayal—it is the ultimate offering to the struggle. It is the paddle to get into the canoe to row to the other side.

Please start building your paddle. Even if it is made out of old, dirty wood you find in a barn. Build your paddle out of your practice, your joy, the things that nourish you. We need you, and we want you to jump in the boat! Plus, I am sure a few of you have already built a whole boat with extra cushions that I would like to jump into.

o   o   o

PHYSICAL DISCOMFORT

There are so many different ways to face our physical pain, to greet it and work within what our abilities are. For many of us, these can change on any given day.

Whether it's chronic illness, something that you were born with, any way that your physical body exists in the world that isn't what is defined as able-bodied: we have a choice to greet ourselves with gentleness.

In the last few years, I've been working through a few different physical body discomforts that have left me feeling completely debilitated—specifically chronic neck and spine pain, fatigue, difficulty with my menstrual cycle, and eczema. It has been uncomfortable, to say the least. Especially when so much of what I am writing about here is about acceptance. I don't want to accept being in pain, feeling like my skin is on fire, or my body not bleeding when I want it to.

I turn toward solutions, I turn toward rest, I turn toward asking for help. Living in the discomfort is really being committed to the both/and of it all. Where do I accept my physical limitations, and where do I seek solutions? And where do I forgive myself when I am too hard on myself or haven't been going toward the things that are good for me?

Getting to center is about going TOWARD center. Some days we never get there. Some weeks it takes a really long time. But we keep going toward it, and when we go away from it, we greet this inaction with self-forgiveness and gratitude that our mind is in awareness.

AS SOMEONE BORN in the midst of what I like to call THE GREAT JUNE MERCURY RETROGRADE OF 1988, I have a special connection with this sweet little transit that comes to us a few times a year. It scares people; it freaks them out. And with a lot of my chart ruled by mercury plus the whole being born in a damn retrograde, I have learned to love it, and how much discomfort comes along with it—and how much magic comes with sitting in it and after.

I have end goals I want to reach, and when I can't reach them on the timeline that I want to, that doesn't work for me. That's when I need to step back to recognize, *Wow, this is so uncomfortable.* I definitely exist in the world with a lot of quickness: I write quickly, I produce quickly, I put things out quickly, I fall in love quickly—I change quickly. So when I don't have access to that sort of fast pivoting, it's really uncomfortable.

Things I do to pivot out of being in discomfort: hydrating, asking for help, sitting meditation, staying really diligent about phone hours, turning the phone off at night, not having it in the bed in the morning—just using the retrograde to realign some of these routines and patterns. But in terms of the greater good of my home, my love, my friendships, the way that people see me, the way that I see myself, my business, my creative practice, my writing practice—feels so stunted. Like I can't just grow past this place that I want to be in.

I turn to acceptance. How do we show up when it just feels really hard? And I say this because there's a separate category of when life is factually hard. Like when you are grieving, when you're in pain, when you are experiencing oppression. There are real ways that life is so difficult for many of us. And I'm speaking more when life is "okay," and you're STILL fighting it. Fighting the timeline that has been divinely planned for you, for me. And thinking, *I have a timeline and it is different from this and I want it to be faster and better and more spectacular.*

At the same time, during many retrogrades I've had spectacular news come to me, and I think, *I'm just still the same person.* And so, I'm working with that too: If I even had what I "wanted" on the timeline that I want, in all these different categories in my life, then what? A little bit of be careful what you wish for. I want to receive exactly what I'm given today. And so I want to show up to my life today, one day at a time. What am I grateful for? Writing a gratitude list, sending gratitude messages, practicing generosity—those are the ways that I'm leaning into the discomfort of not having clarity and not having patience. And deciding to love myself even though I feel both of those things.

I'm not an astrologer, so I don't know what the HELL happens after any given retrograde, but I always know I'll be hanging on. I'm going to be hanging on for all weather. And I'm going to show up for all weather. And know that it's not going to be the same. It's not all going to be the same. And I can have these daily routines, these daily goals, these hopes for my life, these ways that I want to manifest peace and joy and harmony in my life and it's just not going to always go as fast or as easefully as I want it to. And that's okay. I pray for blessings and lessons and discomfort and ease in all astrological weather.

o o o

ALLEVIATING CREATIVE DISCOMFORT

or how we know literally nothing and everything is always changing and no day is the same as the one before it

Sadness usually comes to me when I really think I know something, when I am so, so certain, and then the truth changes and I am left with my unmet expectations. It's also the feeling I most associate with "not wanting to do anything"—sadness that makes me feel like I'm not allowed to talk about creative advising/my work/etc.

This is where we get to do things differently. We can pay attention to the MOMENT we are certain, and then find deep freedom in knowing it could change at any moment. As soon as I am "sure," I should be swift to remember I know nothing, that nothing is in my control (except maybe how much water I drink in a day)

Many days I find myself having my own expectations of certainty shattered. And what a sweet void to be left in! I mean, it's incredibly uncomfortable, but again and again I find I can still show up to my art and writing in this painful discomfort.

SO HOW DO WE DO IT? HOW DO WE SHOW UP THROUGH THE DISCOMFORT/ EVER CHANGING/ALWAYS NEWNESS

o   o   o

How to Alleviate Creative Psychic Discomfort

Daily commitments

Weekly commitments

Adding ease to your practice

Introducing non-negotiables

Self-forgiveness

Connecting to your art community

Staying hopeful

Being of service

Silence

Ask for help

Take a rest

Rearrange

BE WILLING TO PIVOT

o o o

THE DISCOMFORT OF FEELING FROZEN

IF YOU'RE FROZEN, TURN YOUR INNER FREEZE INSIDE OUT.

In hopelessness comes grief and then action. If you're feeling the weight of the world, that's good; that means you haven't numbed out yet to the pain of constant horrors we see on our feeds, television, news, and more.

SOME THINGS THAT help me unfreeze:

o Find someone/an organization that is doing the work around what is impacting my heart and my rage—

read about it, share it, and donate money where
applicable

○ Consider someone in my life who may be directly
affected by a triggering news event: i.e., someone
affected by gun violence, fire destruction, white
supremacy, homophobia—reach out to them and
see how they are and offer a listening ear, send them
money or a service that will uplift their own daily
struggle to exist

○ Take a fucking nap because if I am napped I am more
apt to unfreeze

○ Remember that the social media grid is a tool to share
and uplift, but it is not proof of your or anyone else's
validity in social change

○ Keep making my art, keep writing my books, keep
doing what I was called to do, because not doing
it doesn't stop any of the very bad things from
happening

Very good news I try to also remember that gets me back
to my center in the midst of discomfort: WE NEVER GRADUATE
FROM THE SCHOOL OF REAL LIFE.

CHAPTER 14

Rejuvenation

To rejuvenate is to restore. To rejuvenate is to rest and re-charge. It has been one of the hardest lessons for me to learn, to give myself the gift and full permission to beam brighter, to find my way back to myself through joy and life-giving and rewards.

So much of how I return to my center is through hard work, looking at the inner landscape, asking questions to my shadow self and my past selves and my future selves, envisioning what I want to be and how I want to move through the world.

But when this is done on an everyday basis—I am tired. To be awake is tiring. To be committed is exhausting. To do any of these things and hold any marginalized identities, particularly layered ones, is facing survival and self-care at a level many of us will never know.

So we rest. We find ourselves again and again in states of coming back to ourselves through play, self-care, and adven-ture.

Spring of 2019 was the first time as my own boss where I took a trip that had nothing to do with work. Jackie and I were building a strong friendship before we entered into partnership, and she invited me to visit her in Denver for a few days. Every time I had visited any city ever, I'd planned SOMETHING. A reading, a workshop, a dance class. I would schedule time to write, create content. Working was a means of travel, and one that still feels good to me and sustainable. Getting to work anywhere means I can go anywhere, but it also means I can overwork anywhere and forget to rest.

I thought, *Oh, great! I will visit Jackie and I will plan a book reading and teach a dance class.* And then it occurred to me: What if I went and didn't do a single public event? A city where I could easily sell out a class or fill a room with listeners, a place I've never taught. But what if, just this once—I went with zero plans, zero expectations, and the only commitment to work was to send out my Monday newsletter as planned.

I did this. And I was rejuvenated. I was met with an abundance of friendship. Specifically, I found I was making new friends who had NO idea what I did with my life. They simply loved me because of what I said and what I thought and our shared activities in the moment. By saying no, I was saying yes, to myself and to my relationships. I was giving myself a chance to see a new place, a new landscape, and see myself in it, without any of the performative considerations I often give an experience.

I didn't post on social media while I was there; I kept my interactions close to my own heart and to myself. Each day I learned about new parts of myself, and I didn't have to be on an introspective retreat with a high-ticket price to do that. By all means, invest in yourself and your business and your self-care—but remember that just four days away from working and documenting can bring you back to yourself.

IN THE WINTER of 2019, I purchased a sauna for our home. Other than my 1998 Jeep Cherokee Classic, I believe this is the most expensive object I have ever purchased. In purchasing this object, it took me months and months to even decide it was an "acceptable" purchase. With rejuvenation comes building new stories for ourselves about what is life-giving, what is important to us.

Sweating is important to me. Addressing my anxiety and depression is important to me. Being more available to the world is important to me. Relaxing is important to me. Investing in my relaxation is important to me.

Of course, with any investment of self-care or mental and physical survival, shame and guilt arise. My biggest question to myself was, *Could I have invested this money elsewhere? To an organization that is working to better the world? To an artist who I believe in?*

Yes. Sure, absolutely. But it has been my experience that by focusing on my own rejuvenation, my ability to access productivity and focus comes more easily to me. And this means making more money, having more attention, having more mental energy to learn and grow and be more able to take in the hard truths of the world.

Also, in any house I live in, I host artists. It has been this way for more than a decade. If a touring band is coming through,

I'm hosting resident artists. Someone comes for dinner, they now have a sauna too. We all have a sauna now. When I invest in things for myself, I can share them with anyone else who comes into my world. When I have a working vehicle, I love that I can get to the people and the places I care about. When I rejuvenate, we all rejuvenate.

These are "reasons" for giving yourself permission to do nice things for yourself. But I think it can also be said that rest, relaxation, recharging, and recreation do not need to be categorized into WHY they are important. Or WHY you deserve them. While it is helpful to me to see the benefits of what some might deem "excessive or unnecessary" (I am also talking to my past self from not that long ago), it is also important to remember that we don't need to deserve rest or rejuvenation, we can just have it. It is ours to take and to enjoy.

The idea of "deserving" rest or vacation comes from capitalism—from the idea that we have to work hard in order to deserve, well, anything. But how often are we shown examples from people who don't work hard at all, but seem to have everything? And how many of us become trapped in a cycle of working ourselves to the bone, while still not allowing the joy of a break to come into our lives?

It took me years after first developing the zine *How to Not Always Be Working* to actually take that first "vacation." So if you're on what seems to be a slow journey to understanding your own boundaries and permissions around rest, be easy on yourself! It's hard to undo the lessons we've been taught around being deserving of . . . anything good!

o o o

MAKE A LIST

What are your favorite ways to rejuvenate? What are your favorite ways to rest?

Consider giving yourself full permission; make it exactly how you want it to look.

Physical Rejuvenation

- Sauna
- Bath
- Lie on my acupressure mat
- Go be alone somewhere
- Go be with other people somewhere
- Take a trip and not work for three days

If we're looking at restoring ourselves, this could also look like what some might call "guilty" pleasures. I prefer to take guilt off the table and just call them "pleasures."

This could look like watching a few episodes of your favorite TV show, reading a trashy novel, reading a well-written novel, going to the movies, listening to pop music, etc.

Rejuvenation for me is also about paying attention to my own rhythms, bodily and mentally. When I am going too fast or too slow. Learning to listen to my body and to my mind in terms of what it needs. This hasn't been easy for me (see the chapter on distraction), but it's important to me.

I talked before about noticing when you are reaching for something that might be a distraction. I think rejuvenation is often this tipping point, a rejuvenating moment could sometimes be seen as a distraction depending on my self-judgment versus my self-compassion.

I find when I look at myself with compassion rather than judgment, I have a greater ability to see when something is a distraction or when something is a rejuvenation moment. Earlier I mentioned sex/intimacy with a partner/intimacy with self. This, one of my favorite activities, is something I will often desire when I need a break or I want to reset. It might come from a desire to escape a current feeling or pivot from a task, but it's one that sends endorphins and good feelings through my physical body. Activating my mind! Let yourself orgasm, friends! Let it happen, do it at an inconvenient time, do it any- time, do it so that you can open your eyes wide open and say, YES, I AM READY TO GO! Take a nap afterward, hold your per- son, hold yourself, return to work.

o   o   o

ON GOING OUTSIDE

Going outside is an important practice for me. Someone laughed at me recently when I said it was a practice, but I call it that because I have to constantly remember to go outside. It can be so easy for me to want to stay inside all day. But there is no such thing as bad weather, only bad clothes! This winter I thrifted a down coat for fifteen dollars and have been wearing my fleece-lined leggings under my pants even on the not-so- cold days, just so there is no chance I will want to avoid going outside. Even a fifteen-minute walk brings me back to my center, back to my sense of self.

I started running and exercising a bit. Nothing too wild. I got an app that tells me to run for about a minute at a time before I am allowed to walk again. This has been good for me because I have never in the last ten years managed to run three miles without stopping at least once. But I was honest with myself that I wasn't going to be able to do that. It felt silly to use the app and start so small, but that's why we start small! What a gift to build up to something! Slowly but surely!

I also think I was under the impression that exercising wasn't cool. So much of diet and fitness culture is built on some idealized standard of beauty, and if I exercised, I was giving in to something I didn't believe in. Well, first of all, this is what the business of exercising has done. The images of models or "fit" people the media shows us every day. It's scary, and it is my deep hope and prayer that whatever body image stuff you are processing is gentle. But I also want to tell you that it has been an excellent form of rejuvenation for me. To throw the shoes on and go for a run.

Okay, time-out, though—I am making it sound too easy. This was one of the last chapters I wrote. I wrote this book to teach myself what I wanted to share with you. And it took me writing every other part to know this part. To know that going outside and getting my heart rate up could save my life. That's what rejuvenating does—it saves our lives! And exercising is no different from every other single thing we have to learn to take back for ourselves. To find a gym or a yoga studio or a dance class that reflects back to you the bodies and visions of aliveness you want to see, that you see in yourself.

Consumerism has turned so many good things into twisted, bad things. Eating salads is great! Diet culture is shit! You know what else is great? When I eat a bunch of Oreos and have brown stuff all over my teeth and then have a mini sugar high and can't stop laughing. You also know the phrase "live, laugh, love"? What a cheesy, stupid phrase. Except it's brilliant because if you don't have those three things, what are you even doing?

With rejuvenation, we have to see where societies narratives that we have decided to reject are actually first rooted in being good for us. Only you can decide what is good for you. And only I can decide what is good for me. But unraveling stories of what we are told is part of this. Ideas around work and worth that I learned growing up muddled my idea of who was deserving of rest and relaxation.

This has prevented my ability to accept rest and rejuvenation in my own life. Where do I need to rewrite the script? To heal this part of my self and my ancestral lineage. To show myself that saving and having money isn't bad, it's a part of being human. It's a part of what helps me to access freedom that I can then pass on to others.

o   o   o

THE SLOWNESS OF REJUVENATING

All of 2019, I saw more than ever that I have been finding myself having fun, relishing in the slow Wi-Fi of the rural places I travel to, finding solace in slowing down. Slowing down doesn't have to mean going slow, though. I often find myself going at high speeds in my work and my self-care and my worldviews. They are changing fast, and I am moving rapidly. But I can find slowness and I can find silence, even when there is noise. This used to seem so backward to me. A lot of what I have suggested thus far has to do with action, motion, noise, but there is also much to be learned about chosen silence.

Part of getting to our center is finding our expressive selves, finding when it is time to speak up and to be a much-needed voice in the world of art, injustice, change, and shifting.

But there is also power in silence. Power in holding back, in pausing, in caring for ourselves in ways that aren't easily tracked. You see, the thing about getting to center and returning to ourselves is, it's not linear. It's a spiral and it's a circle and it's one of those dot games you used to play in math class where you connect the dots, but it's not always in the order you thought it might be. It's in a new order, and a new future is being built. If you feel like you're going slower than other people, it's because you might be. And thank goodness. I bet those speedy people are going to look at you and wish they could slow down.

Your pace of birth and rebirth and your ever-changing process is only for you to decide. You have to strengthen your own inner voice to see what is there and what it needs. Talk to yourself, sit in silence, sit in gratitude—this will recharge and restart you. It's scary. It sucks. Being silent and noticing silence can be one of the loudest things we can experience. But I promise it will recharge you in ways you have yet to see come true.

o   o   o

REJUVENATION OF PRAYER

Prayer is a way back to ourselves, and prayer is whatever you say prayer is. Prayer feels like another topic or issue that is ours to reclaim. It is for us to redefine and build our own rituals and structures around. For centuries, we have seen people take beautiful histories of rejoicing and prayer and turn them into weapons of hate. We don't have to do that today, though, just because someone else did.

In times of my deepest darkness, I found two ways to bring myself back to my center: calling a trusted friend or mentor who was able to listen and prayer. When I wake up and get on my knees and pray for a good day, it usually works out pretty well. It's not that the day is automatically magical, but I can sort of source back to that moment and do a 360 spin when shit starts to go haywire.

I make the decision to kneel in prayer because it was suggested to me once and I took it and it worked. If you're like, *Wow, Marlee, what the hell? That seems a little extreme* . . . Is it? If your form of prayer or spirituality is getting you through, I hope you keep doing it, and I hope you keep doing it every day.

To me, a state of prayerful kneeling keeps me in tune with the floor, which is connected to the ground, which is connected to me. I also don't really envision it as praying TO something else as much as honoring myself, kneeling before my past and future selves to say, *I see you, I am with you, I am with the universe, and today I want to remember how to get back to myself when I might stray.*

Because most days, I will stray. I will try to abandon myself. Even if it's just for five or ten minutes. Prayer throughout the day is also the way back to myself. I have always loved Anne Lamott's book *Help, Thanks, Wow,* her offering to us that these could be the only three prayers we need. To ask for help, to be grateful, and to be in awe are states I want to access with the help of divine guidance. To rejuvenate is to say what is and to say what isn't and to not hate myself on the journey of finding it all out.

o   o   o

REJUVENATION OF AWE AND NEW LOVE

WHEN WE ARE OFF OUR CENTERS FROM THE WHIRLWIND OF NEWNESS

Throughout this book I speak of love. My ability to fall in and out, the way it knocks us off our centers—sometimes deeper into the abyss and sometimes deeper into states of joy.

I don't think falling in love the way I do is bad. But I have seen the ways where I become disconnected from self because I have put something or someone before my prayer practice, which is the same as my self-practice.

There are a few instances where I truly believe I fell in love at first sight. A wild feeling of connection and my heart exploded and I was in love. And while I thought it was with the other person, I actually think it might have just been with myself. Or these instances have reflected to me how I see myself now. It's the sort of love that maybe isn't real because it's so new. It's the way I'm immediately in love with a good patch of roses coming out of a sidewalk crack and no one asks me twice about loving those so swiftly.

This is where I think love can rejuvenate us, even if it knocks us off our centers completely. Getting away from center isn't bad, it's just another part of the road map where we get to build it back. Whether your new wild love becomes your forever mate, or only lasts through one more blizzard, it can still be one of your greatest teachers about yourself.

CHAPTER 15

Guilt/Saying No as a Form of Self-Love

My 2019 commitment was to experience joy without guilt. I carry guilt around making money, a discomfort in comfort. I carry survivor's guilt about being an addict who didn't die. I carry guilt as an obsession that blocks me from my relationship to joy, which is the same as my relationship to god, which is the same as my relationship to everything.

I've been practicing boundless and wild joy. It seems to pair well with dips of grief for me, but I think feeling the grief of letting go is part of what makes the joy so sweet. It's not that I didn't feel joy before, but it was just that joy and comfort made me want to hide, not show you or myself how magical it could all be—being alive. I've learned that I can experience joy and still be mad at the world. I can experience joy and still be of service. I can still take action. I can experience joy and still honor the circumstances around me where others might be affected.

Shrinking my own joy to make others feel more comfortable doesn't serve any of us. So I vow to stay committed to experiencing mine in an effort to bring us all to the other side, where it flows freely and without guilt.

I also find it helpful to find joy teachers. Some that I look to are Shira Erlichman, Jacqueline Suskin, Jamila Reddy, Megan Touhey, Brandi Harper, and many more. People who I know are walking through the world and facing the hard pains, and still choosing joy no matter what knocks them off their centers.

I am often the farthest from my center when I have passed a deadline, emails are piled up, I've sabotaged my finances again, I'm not doing the simple maintenance things to take care of myself, and therefore I am not letting myself access the things that usually shift me out of this: radical self-care, movement, plant allies, my work, my creative practice.

This is how guilt and shame manifest in my life. As a total freeze up, the inability to do anything. Guilt and shame live together in a little bubble inside of my head. They've made themselves a nice, cozy zone to lie around in all day and tell me I am a miserable failure—*Why even start if you are going to fail like you have in the past?*

First of all, what even IS failing? Who made this word up? They're an asshole—don't listen to them. Something not going as planned does not mean that you failed. It means that you weren't ready yet, that something different was in line with the universe.

So when I am past a deadline, instead of beating the living shit out of myself due to the level of guilt and shame I feel, I can get curious. I can notice. I can ask myself: What threw me so far off center that I can't seem to even feel my feet on the ground?

I take pen to paper and I make a list. I am Harriet the Spy and I am a detective and I will get to the bottom of this. Sometimes the answer just wants to be "I am depressed" or "I am sad" or "I am feeling a lot of grief."

But I can also go deeper, look at the pathways that took me there, look at the pathways to get back to myself and back to my center. This is hard work. It's exhausting. And we can also remember that it is a practice and when we practice something enough times, it does start to get easier. And we can always return. Cutting through the shame and the guilt can be a full-time job, though. Don't fool yourself! Be easy if it doesn't feel like you can access it.

Shame is a painful feeling. It is in our bodies. It creates a wave of destruction through our hearts and our minds and paralyzes us from action. For me, this wave emerges almost exclusively from "Why haven't I figured this out YET?"

o   o   o

Things I Tell Myself I Will Never Figure Out:

How to be in a healthy relationship
My taxes
Healing my debt
Doing my bookkeeping
Budgeting
Being a good friend
Being an artist
Finishing things on time

Folding my clothes

Doing the dishes right after I've used them

Exercising

Calling people back in a timely manner

A consistent morning routine

Consistency, in general really

Self-forgiveness

Stretching

Replying to emails

Drinking enough water

Remembering to take baths

o o o

THIS LIST, WHEN I look at it, is so mean to myself. The things I listed are literally what being a human is. This is where the comparison spiral of the digital sphere comes in, this idea that we are supposed to be a finished product, that there is this MOMENT where we are complete. Where we are totally finished "fixing" the parts of ourselves that are off-kilter. That are off center.

Centering is about transformation. It's about a continued practice. It's about a continued curiosity. It's the forever commitment to returning, not the idea that one day we'll have put all the pieces into place.

When I look at this list, I feel shame. I feel the guilt of having a career that helps other people navigate similar topics, but who am I to speak on them when I haven't gotten anything figured out? Anything is a long shot. I have a few things figured out. And many things on this list I have done with consistency and vigilance. And they go in phases of how easy it is for me to get to them. It's a story in my mind that I am not worthy of sharing my in-process truth.

I can also remind myself in a shame spiral all of the things I have figured out! Like how to not take a drink in nine years, sending my newsletter out every Monday, working hard at my first long-term partnership in a few years, becoming a dog mom, learning how to cook new things.

I also often choose fun, creative projects, social activities, and rest instead of the things on my list. And attaching guilt to those is the result of living in a world that celebrates the hustle and productivity hacks, instead of rest and naps and careful consideration of our bodies and minds and habits.

So how do we release it?

One thing I realized was that the loud voice screaming at me about guilt and shame in my head was just trying to get my attention. It had been being soft, going through phases of being kind and loving. *Be nice to Marlee, treat her well, get her in the bathtub, let her sit down to write and not try to grab her phone every few minutes.*

When I ignore this soft nudge for long enough, it gets loud and it gets mean and it shames me. Not because it hates me, though—because it loves me. Because it wants me to be well and to create structure and to try again. And my insistence on not listening blocks me from my true self. The soft voice says, *Let's try this again. Let's make a list. You can do this—I am sure of it.* But I choose to ignore this because after enough waves of self-guilt I have decided that kind of softness isn't for me. I am not worthy of it. So the voice gets louder, until I am just a miserable ball of shame mush. Waiting to be blended into a viscose and served for dinner. But the voice is just trying to get my attention.

Shame comes from ignoring my feelings. It comes from the never-ending spiral of feeling humiliation based on a series of things I would like to be good at or not "mess up" at. And instead of turning toward the curious soft voice within me that can ask questions about why this comes up—I often turn to negative self-talk that turns the loop into a loud, mean, never-ending quest to prove to myself that I am bad.

I see this manifest in physical intimacy with partners. Society teaches us that sexual desire is the ultimate form of acceptance and care and stability in a partnership. That to be physically intimate with a romantic partner is an ultimate form of acceptance. I take this so far away from the centering nature of my relationship that it can also put a pressure on what should be fun and nourishing to a partnership. If a partner doesn't want to have sex and I do, it is my responsibility to make them feel safe in their not wanting to. Consent goes both ways, and making a safe space for these conversations proves fruitful in the long run.

When I take a denial of my advances personally and go into a state of irritability or coldness, this does not create a space for conversation, compromise, or quality communication. I relate all of this to shame because this is serious unlearning I have had to do, and it goes beyond sex. Really, when anything doesn't go "my way" or the way I have deemed "correct," it is my natural state to lash out. Or lash inward and be uncommunicative, icy, shut down.

As soon as I recognize it, which at this point I find to be almost instantaneous from doing so much of the work presented in this book, I am consumed with shame. How could I, a queer person with good consent practice and care, be so cold to someone I love so much? A bigger question that arises that shame can teach me is: How did I get so far away from my own center that I could create this level of discord with someone I love? This goes for platonic relationships, artistic collaborations, and so forth.

So I face my options. I can listen to my shame. I can see what this shame is trying to bring up for me. It's usually saying, *You are better than this*. But it goes awry when it says, *You are better than this and YOU SHOULD HAVE DONE better than this*. That's where I greet the shame demon in my mind and say, *I hear you*. Because I so often try to just get rid of it. *GO AWAY, SHAME. I don't want you here. I don't want you anywhere near me*.

I try to throw it out of the car. I want so badly to be in the driver's seat, but Shame Marlee is a worthy passenger, creeping in from time to time to ask me to pivot my emotions.

The other fear I hold around shame is I feel it's a signal that I have done something so wrong that people will leave me. I will be abandoned. I will be left to figure this out on my own. No partnership, family member, or friendship could possibly withstand this mess up—and my shame is here to prove it.

However, in my humble thirty-two years of being alive, I have found this to be both true and not true. People will leave us. They will, I'm sure of it. And new people come into their place. And the new people usually have a higher level of being able to withstand our mistakes, our mess ups, whatever we deem too much to show another person. We are surrounded by mirrors, and we should be so lucky. And we should be so lucky to continue to see who sticks around.

○   ○   ○

PROTECTION SPELL FOR GUILT/ SHAME OF A RELATIONSHIP GONE

Okay, maybe this isn't a spell, it's more like a pep talk, but I'd like to walk us through something that I have been deeply processing in my adult life, which is the end of a friendship/collaborative relationship/internet follower/anything nonromantic.

A lot of what I explore in this book applies to this moment, but I want to speak to it in a pointed and specific way. It could, like much of what I write about, be filed away under the "uncool" thing to talk about. Which is what shame does to us. It decides what is cool or not cool to talk about. And it usually haunts us over the things that, if we DID indeed talk about them, would set us free.

In relationships of the romantic nature, we give so much more grace. Because of COURSE you will feel pain, on both sides. We have given ourselves societal permission to feel natural guilt for ending a relationship, shame if you did something wrong. We find ways to navigate this with how much help there is out there for romantic partnerships ending.

But when it comes to a friendship or business relationship, or now in the digital age an internet follower you maybe don't even KNOW! We start to get really afraid and sad that . . . get ready for it . . . WE ARE FRAUDS.

IF SOMEONE DOESN'T LIKE ME = I AM A FRAUD

AN IMPOSTER OF A GOOD PERSON

TWO FAILED FRIENDSHIPS = INABILITY TO BE A FRIEND TO ALL

And it's all on you. Especially if this person has told everyone how fucked-up/problematic/bad you were. They must be right, and you must be wrong.

Well, from the bottom of my own damn barrel, I am here to report: this is not true, and we must smash it with a hammer. We must smash it like a geode that looks like a normal-ass rock, and then when you destroy it you find out that there's a fucking crystal inside of it.

YOU ARE THE CRYSTAL INSIDE OF AN UGLY ROCK.

(Okay, no rock is ugly, all rocks are perfect, because they are from Earth, but you get it. It looks like just another old thing on the ground, but it is not.)

So, you, my dear, sweet, perfect angel of a human on Earth, are worthy of new friendships. You are worthy of loving and liking yourself. You are worthy of new readers and new companions and new collaborators. The people who don't like you aren't bad. And you aren't bad for not being able to maintain a relationship with them.

o o o

ON HARM/AMENDS/WRONGDOING/ ACCOUNTABILITY (AND THEN WE'LL GET TO THE DAMN PROTECTION SPELL)

I don't condone just throwing your hands up and thinking,

WELP, THEY DON'T LIKE ME ANYMORE. This feels like an anger mask for guilt and shame. It's easier to think, *GONNA CUT THIS CORD—BYE-BYE,* than to look within and see where we weren't accountable to ourselves or other people. Do that first. Before we go into protection and cutting the cord, ask yourself: *What was my part? Where did I not stay committed to my own course or what we had set out to do together?*

And then, if an amends should be made, make them. First, ask them if they are willing to receive it. We don't make amends about what the other person did; we make them about our actions. If that person still doesn't want to remain friends, or worse yet, deems you unsafe/problematic/unworthy of love from any person and either holds that to themselves or spreads it around, we take new action.

This is nuanced. It's hard to talk about. As soon as BIG words get thrown around—"Gaslighting," "abuse," "unsafe"—it's really scary to hear those things about yourself. Even if it's from one person.

My ex-girlfriend once told me I was gaslighting her around something she was feeling, and it was HORRIFYING. I thought, *There is absolutely no way that I could be that kind of monster. ONLY monsters do that.* But I took a deep breath and listened to her and held her vulnerability. I felt so much shame, but also so much gratitude that she was able to stand in her voice and tell me that. While our romantic relationship ended, our friendship stands strong.

Building vulnerability with others where you can share when they are being hurtful is a part of how we all get stronger.

Okay! On to protecting ourselves.

People aren't going to like you. They're gonna think you totally suck. They're gonna hate your art and your boyfriend and your stupid tote bag and they're gonna laugh at your IGTV or your YouTube channel.

And you're gonna feel like a stupid baby. AND THEN YOU'RE GONNA FEEL LIKE AN ETHERAL QUEEN WITH THE CROWN OF ALL THAT IS GOOD INSIDE YOU.

Get a candle, any candle. I like a black protection candle from Mother Moon, a witch store by the beach in Saugatuck, MI.

Add pictures of people who love you, and a picture of yourself, who is so awesome.

Take mountain pennyroyal, a flower essence for protection against outside energies having opinions about you.

Get your favorite rocks from the yard and THE STAR tarot card

Sit in front of this altar. Ask for divine guidance. Ask to step into your power. Remember that people leaving you leaves so much more room for the right people to come in. Those are your people. Take better care of yourself and of them.

Shame can also sneak in when I attach my worth to things outside of myself. My expectations go up for everyone around me. My partner, my friends, my students, my mentors. I want everyone to step up because maybe then, just then, I would feel less irritable. The loop begins—my irritability comes out of me in words, and then the people I want to nourish the most get irritable, and then I'm just more irritable.

So I pause. I sit to write. I take a shower. I read my goddamn Melody Beattie codependency daily reflection books. Then I try not to overthink *What's wrong with me?* or *What "problem within me" can I solve today?*

o   o   o

PRAYER FOR SHAME AND GUILT

LET SHAME FALL AWAY!

SHAME IN THE LITTLE THINGS WILL WEAR YOU OUT

YOU ARE A MIRACLE!

PAUSE FOR FIVE MINUTES TODAY JUST TO BE QUIET, JUST TO BE STILL, JUST TO SAY THANK YOU

SAY THANK YOU TO YOURSELF, FOR STAYING ANOTHER DAY

When I am spiraling, I remember:

Miracles! Miracles! A simple day of witnessing Earth is a true miracle!

It's miraculous, y'all, just to be here on the spinning rock, and I promise to keep remembering this simple joy amidst the crushing darkness!

CHAPTER 16

Ease

You are working so hard at all of this. At self-awareness, at staying on the beam. Making it easy for ourselves is an amazing way to stay connected and committed to self. Exploring ways to release the shame of pleasure and reward and magic of ease—with this knowing that by creating ease for ourselves, we just might be able to create ease for others.

Experiencing the world is not easy—it simply is not.
Most people reading this book picked it up because
they have not or have never had an easy time, moreso
than others. It is rare that a white, straight cis man
reads or interacts with my work. If this is your identity
and you are reading this—WELCOME! WE NEED YOU!
We need you to do this work with us and stay soft
and tend to your femininity and tender masculinity.

However, most of you who read this are:

- Womxn
- Nonbinary
- BIPOC
- Trans folx
- Poor
- Working-class
- People with disabilities
- Fat
- Deaf
- Neurodivergent
- Queers
- And any combination of the above

I love you! I see you! The world does not want it to be easy for us, and it does not want us to have access to what we need to access ease.

So we must create this access for ourselves and for one another. And when we build ease into our own lives, we build ease into all of our lives. It is an act of service, an act of restoration, reparative and restorative and responsible.

Why do we avoid ease? Class shame, the idea that rest and ease are deserved. That things can be easeful only if we have suffered or are in pain. We must leave this concept behind. This is where the fear of jealousy comes in, or the idea that confidence makes you look cocky. We have to get rid of these too. We have to keep moving, smashing the idea that our success blocks other people from theirs.

I hope you all stay confident and make a shit-ton of money. Money creates ease, for yourself and others. Redistribute your wealth, donate to local charities, create a scholarship fund for your workshop or service, fund-raise for something with your extra time. These are ways to make ease for yourself that transmutes into ease for others. Because the world does not, I repeat, does not want ease for us.

Actually, I take that back. God is everything, and the Spirit of the Universe has so much ease and grace within it—constantly begging us to be soft and thoughtful. A two-party-system government, a heteronormative patriarchy, white supremacy—these systems were built to oppress us, to not be easeful. So we rest. We create ease. We build in days off. We drink our water. Otherwise, we burn out. And when we burn out, we get resentful, sad, sick, unavailable, and in pain. We are as far from our center as we can get, because that is what the system is designed to do—to knock us as far off as we can get.

Ask for help—you cannot do everything yourself. Yet everyone feels shame around asking for help. Recognize the support systems you have around you, and lean on them and get comfortable asking for help. It's okay to spend money—get a Lyft if you're going to have an anxiety attack on the subway. This is giving permission and exploring what's "worth" it.

I also notice so many folks feeling guilt around hiring help! Hiring an assistant, teammates, someone to help you ship orders. This is where creating ease for yourself means providing jobs for others! It means your work reaches more people—and we never know who our work is for, so we must show up for the process. Why not make it easier?

o o o

AVOIDING INTIMACY WITH SELF

I have noticed that when I am in unease or DIS-ease, I am in avoidance of something, and more often than not, I am avoiding intimacy with myself. What if I let intimacy with myself be easy? Could I just decide that it was easy? In the constant state of reaching for the phone, for anything to lose myself in the whirlwind of the not-present moment, I am avoiding intimacy with myself.

For so long I found this very confusing. I find it very easy to be intimate with others, almost too quickly sometimes. Sharing so much of myself with them, my deepest vulnerabilities, my greatest fears. I'll fall in love, I'll show them the whole me, but do I really? How can I actually show someone the whole me if I'm not looking at the whole me?

I love to SEE my Jackie in her wholeness, and she reflects back to me how seen she feels. But it's easy for me to rely on that as my way of seeing myself, she is often a mirror for me. But this is not the same as looking within, as looking deep within myself.

MY NEW FAVORITE TRICK TO PUT MY PHONE DOWN, PUT WHATEVER IS CONSUMING ME DOWN (this could be physically or energetically): I take a very deep breath as early into the process as possible and I ask myself, *Am I avoiding being intimate with myself?* The answer is always yes.

o   o   o

Ways to Be Intimate with Myself in a Crisis Spiral in Fifteen Minutes or Less:

- Lie on the ground and take deep breaths and do nothing
- Meditate for three minutes (not even TEN—REALLY, JUST THREE, FOR GOD'S SAKE)
- Do nothing
- Masturbate
- Put my hand on my heart and take three deep breaths
- Take a shower
- Drink a big glass of water
- Journal
- Draw a picture of what's inside my brain
- Make a pie chart of my thoughts
- Put my feet in the dirt

Longer Ways of Creating Intimacy with Self:

- Take a walk
- Swim
- Baths

Make these lists for yourself and keep them close as a re-centering practice.

o o o

ANCESTRAL EASE

When you are faced with this *What is the point?* idea around your work and your practice and your visions—remember that we are doing the work for everyone who came before us who could not. Our ancestors are hoping we heal what they could not. And this is where our practice of being alive goes so far beyond our art making and our business and our work—with the availability that it can also be integrated at the same time.

So much of what we do every day is both an offering to our ancestors as well as a way to collaborate with them. It is also an opportunity to BE good ancestors, to carve out a better way for whoever comes next.

o   o   o

Be Committed to Looking Inward

Therapy, psychic counseling, journaling, twelve steps
Researching and understanding bias—if you are white-
 bodied or white-passing, finding a class, book, or
 organization to become educated about antiracism.
  *My Grandmother's Hands: Racialized Trauma and
   the Pathway to Mending Our Hearts and Bodies*
   by Resmaa Menakem—a book that helped me
   understand how racism lives in my body
  Educator and writer Rachel Cargle's Patreon,
   articles, and Instagram account have all helped
   me see where I fall short, with direct ways to
   shift that behavior. You can send her money and
   subscribe to her Patreon.
  *A City Within a City: The Black Freedom Struggle
   in Grand Rapids, MI*—it's helpful to find a book
   about the history of where you came from and
   how that has impacted your view of the world

and people in it

Action steps to re-distribute wealth and resources to trans folx, Black people, poor folks, indigenous people, people with disabilities.

You can take steps to redistribute your wealth and resources to trans, Black, and poor people, and people with disabilities—this can look like one, five, or five hundred dollars to organizations locally or globally that are doing work you believe in

o   o   o

THESE ARE ALL things you CAN integrate into your art practice and business, but they are also just how to be a good person who can use privilege and voice to understand self and others. This is where DECENTERING yourself is a practice of ease. By getting out of the center, you can create easeful spaciousness for other voices.

At the same time, we face this idea around having a platform or influence—if you know one other human, you have this gift. You don't have to have thousands of followers or even a hundred dollars to make an impact with your words and your voice. In fact, by using your voice, or quieting it for the space of others, you carve out an energy field that will attract the right people.

I found that when I started digging into what it meant for me to carefully asses my biases inwardly—internalized racism, homophobia, ableism—my whole world started changing. To rid myself of white guilt or savior complex, to see where I had let society teach me things that were untrue, became a point of study and necessary research that lead me to a deeper understanding of self and others. Ways I wanted to lean into "diversity" as a public person instead of leaning into: Who do I want to get to know and have in my world? How could we enrich and learn from each other? That is when I started to see my outer world match my inner values.

It can be painful to admit you have learning and unlearning to do. But we need you to learn with us! Find resources in your local community, and on the internet! Find teachers (and pay them), zines, books, online workshops—you have everything you need to do this work, I promise. And once you do, you will see the people and opportunities and magic around you shift— because YOU are shifting.

o o o

PRAYER FOR EASE FOR OTHERS

May we allow ease to flow into our hearts
May we remember that ease for the self
may allow ease for those around us
We will release shame and guilt around ease
We will be generous with the resources
that come to us through our own ease

CHAPTER 17

Hope

If you've made it this far into the book, you've looked at yourself. You've looked deeply into the wounds that live in your body. I write today to pledge to end smallness. To end fear. To end the part of me that says there is no hope, something that lives in the bones of those who came before me and transferred to me in the womb.

I am in a constant state of unlearning and relearning. Unwinding and unfolding. There is no shortage of discomfort and hopelessness for me to attach to—to become completely obsessed with. It is in the discomfort I am most uncomfortable. It is familiar to me. If I were to change to a state of hopefulness, would I also be required to end the inner suffering and struggle?

So I stay hopeful. I choose to stay hopeful. This does not come naturally to me. My fear of failure comes quickly—I choose this state. I can choose differently, from doing the work and from seeing how many times I have "failed" only to see more miracles on the other side. While I stay hopeful of this lifetime and ones before, I also stay committed to the knowledge that everything could indeed go wrong. Whatever "wrong" is. Not the way I planned. If I could count the times things did not go as planned and turned out so much more astounding than I could ever have imagined, it would be every single thing, every experience. Being alive has been a series of events that have led me to more and more hope and faith in the universe's sweet plan for me.

There are two types of hope I want to address: hope in ourselves, and hope in the collective. What I spoke about above is the first—how do we maintain the hope that we are already complete and that we can keep improving?

The next phase of hope is hope for the collective. They go hand in hand. Hope and faith also go hand in hand.

Sometimes hope is too close to desire. In hope, I long for faith, that everything will turn out exactly as designed. Which may or may not be what I have in mind or what I think I have planned.

I hope for a new leader of our country. I hope for safety for immigrants. I hope for clean water for Flint. I hope for women to get paid the same as men. I hope for trans women of color to stop getting murdered. I hope for addicts to find recovery. I hope for gun control. I hope for pain to dissolve from people I love.

These hopes have a desired outcome. When I hope, I am also praying at the same time. While I always pray for the universe's will over my own, these prayers and hopes come into my mind in a hope for a better world for all of us. There are times when we do put faith in the world and it still seems to come out wrong. Which brings me back to the hope in myself.

When everything is falling down around us, when the systems were created to keep us small and in fear, we MUST stay hopeful in ourselves and our close communities. To be hopeful is to be of service. To have faith in ourselves is to heal ourselves and one another. Without this unwavering belief in our growth, we will let ourselves down, and then we won't be able to be available for others.

How the HELL do we do this? How do we stay hopeful when the world seems dark, our hearts break, people we love die, elections are rigged? When I was trying to get sober, I remember thinking, *I am totally hopeless.* There is no way a drunk like me could ever not take a drink . . . could ever go a day without thinking about taking the next drink. Alas, nine years without a drink and I am reminded that that exact feeling of hopelessness is now my offering of HOPE to the world.

I was twenty-two when I quit drinking, just a few weeks before my twenty-third birthday. I had known I was an alcoholic since I was nineteen years old, and I went to my first AA meeting when I was twenty. But I was certain I was too young. There's no way I could have a drinking problem—I was attending a good university, running a student cooperative organization, hadn't gotten in any legal trouble, and could still mostly show up to things. Alas, I hated myself, and I continued to hate myself in the wake of my drinking and how it would destroy me and everything around me. I would continue to get sicker and sicker, until one day I had lost most of what was important to me.

May 16, 2011, the last day I drank, I didn't get wasted and I didn't black out and I didn't throw up on myself. But I did walk up to my house after having a few drinks, and it's when I had my "god" moment, my white light moment. And this moment came from hope. That some part of me hoped that there could be a different way. I went through the list in my head. *Do I have more booze in the freezer? Should I walk to the store and get more beer? What time do I have to work tomorrow and how busy will it be? Will I be able to hide how drunk I am? Will I have to run to the bathroom to throw up before I take my next table's order?*

The checklist went on, and I paused and looked at my front door, and it hit me—*I don't think most people have to think about this as much as I do.* I didn't drink every day, and I didn't drink every morning, but I thought about drinking every day and every morning when I woke up. I thought about if I would drink or not. Hope for a new life for myself emerged, out of what seemed like thin air, and I had hope in myself. It was this day that was really the beginning of my journey of returning to center, and I'm grateful that I haven't taken a drink since.

We share. This keeps us out of isolation. This keeps us in togetherness. Whether it's with your therapist, your partner, your newsletter, your YouTube channel, a FaceTime with your best friend, we share. Over and over and over. Until we learn it and have to learn it again. Every time I relearn something, I have to retrain my voice from being hateful toward myself to being celebratory.

When I lose hope or faith in myself, I am SO mean to Marlee. The little me inside wants to stay small; she chooses to listen to the voice. I try something new, or something old—and I can't quite tackle it. So instead of being gentle and addressing myself with patience and love, I am just angry and unkind. Not giving myself the patience I try so diligently to cultivate.

○ ○ ○

HOPE IS A PRACTICE

I believe that hope and prayer are practices, that they are actionable. We often don't think of ideas as being actionable. I suppose it could be my hope that you would, just for a moment, consider that you too could turn hope into an action. This could look like setting up an altar, sitting down to say prayers out loud, and inventing your own ways to put hope into action.

PRACTICE: CONVERT HOPELESSNESS TO BENEFIT OTHERS

Write down all the ways you have felt hopeless in the past, and the ways that those feelings are now offerings to those who might benefit from your experience.

PRACTICE: NOTICE

Begin to notice again—blades of grass, clouds, even just one thing. For every small phenomenon that chips away at your hope, notice or write down a true wonder that helps you return to it.

It is a hope practice of mine to put my feet on the earth. Not in my shoes, but barefoot, I return to the earth. Give myself back to the earth. The place I came from. You can look up which Indigenous land you are on, give thanks to those who this land belongs to, prayers for support from the dirt.

o   o   o

Tools

- o Sharing with friends
- o Time with friends tends to be a way that I stay hopeful, especially in seasons with less light and more snow
- o Start things with your friends—book clubs, knitting circles. Can't be together in real life? Try ZOOM or host an Instagram Live talk show.
- o Have potlucks
- o Reallocate money to things you believe in!

o   o   o

GOING TOWARD YOUR FRIENDS WHO MAKE ART

I want to speak more directly to hope and its implications for our careers, our art practices, our ways of showing up to ourselves. Because I think that social media distraction and addiction is a huge part of our hopelessness. The way we interact with Instagram, the way we take in so much information. I want to break down some facts and hopefully make you feel less alone in the pain of it all.

It's a pep talk for 1) people who are addicted to Instagram

and 2) people who run a business on Instagram. If you're nei-ther of those people, go outside, text someone you love, and don't worry about reading this. Skip to a different chapter. Or, actually, maybe keep reading this, because you might not even realize you are one of those people. Or maybe your partner or best friend or collaborator is one of those people and you could be helpful to them. And if you are one of those people—I'm both of those people—then you might get something out of this.

Something I've experienced often is people coming to me—friends, clients, collaborators—who say, "I feel like no one's seeing my Instagram posts. I feel terrible." Then they ask, "Was my dress not cool enough? Is my online class stupid? Am I an asshole?"

These are the questions we are all asking ourselves because of an app on our phone.

One of my favorite books, *How to Break Up with Your Phone* by Catherine Price, addresses the dopamine hits that happen when we are constantly on our phones.

She talks about how we "blame our binges on a lack of will-power." This, of course, puts the blame on ourselves instead of designers at tech companies, who very skillfully design these apps to get responses from our brains that make it extremely hard for us to stop using them.

You look at the feed. You look at your followers. There are thousands. There are TENS OF THOUSANDS. But that's not what our engagement/exchange or rate is, so this phone will also tell you that your attention span is SHOT!

Here's why I share this with you. One day I might post about creative advising. It's a one-on-one service I offer to artists. We strategize, we talk about creative blocks—it's amazing. I'm great at it. People love it. I struggle with sharing about it on social media. So I was like, *I'm gonna push myself, all right?* I post a picture of myself, on a mountain, talk about my feelings—three thousand people love it. Sooo many comments. When I finally posted a picture about creative advising: four hundred people. Right? Gratitude, of course.

You might be thinking, *Four hundred people, that's so many.* Yes, yes, but what the designers of the app have said is, *We're gonna give you thousands of likes on a selfie not selling anything. Then, when we sense that you're trying to tell the people a real way that you could be of service to them, we're not gonna give you that.*

It makes us really spiral out into questions of, *What's happening? Is my online class just terrible? Am I terrible? Is my product terrible? Is my line of stationery dumb?* "No" is the answer to all of those questions.

When we see the large number of likes on the selfie, it's a slot machine! Think about the refresh, the swipes of the stories, the hit after hit after hit—dopamine slam. So we're like, *I got so many likes on the selfie, I'm gonna keep going.* I'm never consciously thinking that this post really nails it for me, that this is gonna be the one that everyone loves. But it's happening subconsciously.

By the time I post about creative advising, it's shot. They're gonna give me nothing. They know, by not showing it to anyone, I'm gonna try again.

So I get vulnerable. I share something I tried—I pulled some prints yesterday, got some new tricks up my sleeve: 280 likes, eighty thousand followers. I didn't even say the words "for sale." It is my theory that Instagram doesn't want me to believe in myself so that in my state of low self-esteem I will continue to engage.

Now I don't believe in myself—just kidding, I totally do, but in the moment that is how I feel. I DO believe in myself because I know it's not me, it's the app designers who have done this to all of us. And this is how I HOPE we return to a collective HOPEFULNESS. That we can really see where this is not us—it's not our abilities, it's not our worth. We are tying so much into the numbers even when we don't realize it.

This my hope for sharing this—it is not to complain. I don't want to complain. I am grateful for my life today. It is why I wrote a zine called *how a photo and video-sharing social networking service gave me my best friends, true love, a beautiful career, and made me want to die."* And I don't mean that dramatically. I mean it especially as an addict—as someone who used to put drugs up their nose and get blackout drunk at the smallest outbreak of feeling.

I want the dopamine hits, and they're keeping us afraid and they're keeping us addicted and it's okay, you're not the only one who feels it. Make your own newsletter, make zines, call your friends, get collaborators, print with ink, get your hands messy, put your feet in the dirt outside, love yourself, take a break, and THEN you can be of service, okay? Don't let it get you down.

o   o   o

Podcasts I Listen to to Access My Own Hope Practice:

- *Living in This Queer Body* with Asher Panjiris
- *Still Processing* with Jenna Wortham and Wesley Morris
- *Queery* with Cameron Esposito
- *On Being* with Krista Tippet

o   o   o

PART OF MY teaching practice revolves around hope. I teach my students to generate more hope in all of us. We always spend the first week visioning the kind of ideal world we would want to live in, both for ourselves and for our community. This homework is often really uncomfortable for people. They want to jump right into the *Well, how do we make our art and change the world?!* I don't believe we can do this without first looking inward to see what kind of world we even hope for.

Scholarships, trades, and payment plans are a huge foundation of my online courses that I teach on creativity, developing habits, and forgiving ourselves. I can see how this financial flexibility allows such a wide range of people to participate in my offerings—we CAN do things differently than big business, and we can do things in a way that stays true to softness and generosity and togetherness. It is this way of doing business that is putting my hope into action. I want to see a world where those who can afford to pay for something at full price help to offset those who are unable to. It has ultimately led to a very joyful class with students across so many different disciplines and lived experiences.

And you can do this too! You can develop your own online offering or class or share your art. I HOPE that you do. And in doing so you can experiment with how your offerings or objects are priced.

Hope really can translate into everything you do, how you work, and what you share. When I feel stuck about what to say or how to synthesize my voice into public format, I often ask myself, *What is it that I hope for? Who do I want justice for?* And do I want it now. This is also how I choose where to donate my money, what organizations to fund-raise for. I tap into my hope—and I lead from that place.

CHAPTER 18

Faith

"Faith has no preconceptions; it is a plunge into the unknown. Belief clings, but faith lets go. In this sense of the word, faith is the essential virtue of science, and likewise of any religion that is not self-deception."

—ALAN WATTS

You have to have faith in yourself! You must! If it's the only thing you take away from this book, I am fine with that. You did a great job, dear reader. You must above all things have faith that you are resilient and you are capable of surviving and of rising above and living brightly.

I am not saying everything will be great and manageable and perfect and the best thing ever. Really bad shit is going to happen to you, around you, to people that you love and never want to hurt. But if you keep the faith in yourself—you will get through. And you will get through with ease and gratitude and be brighter on the other side.

Belief clings! But faith lets go! This has been a foundational element to me in reframing how I trust the people in my life, and the universe's unique and transcendent plan for me. To believe in something is to wish it true, to seek an attached outcome, or a hopeful outcome you might want to see happen.

Faith is the trust that it will turn out exactly as it should. Faith in a person is putting your trust in their goodness. Sometimes I don't believe someone, but I can still have faith. When I am building trust with a new romantic partner or friend—I wish I could just believe what they say. But to build real trust, I have to let myself swim in that in-between state for a while. The state of not knowing, but having faith in their goodness.

This is where I won't tell you to believe in yourself, but to have faith in yourself. When I try to believe in myself, I usually get discouraged. Because my track record has proven that maybe I shouldn't believe in myself. But faith—yes, I have this.

Faith, like many holy words, like the word "holy" itself, tends to get swept up in religious jargon that so many of us deem unfit for our radical lives. But here I am to reclaim it, to bring it back to us in full force on the earthly plane with a direct line to the otherworldly plane. Faith is ours to integrate, but how? How do we have faith?

You may already have a faith practice in place. A religion, a version of god, a universal truth you hold on to. Maybe you integrate new age practices, altar building, movement ritual. There are so many ways to build a faith practice—it's limitless and it is abundant and there is no wrong way.

A faith practice is a way to apply returning to our centers at lightning speed, to close the gap of time between self-hatred, distraction, grief, loss of hope. A faith practice centers us on command, because it is access to knowledge of the utmost knowing: knowing that we don't know and that whatever may be is what will be, and that is goodness in action.

ONE THING I ask myself often is, *Well, what is the center, anyway, and how do you know if you're not in it?*

So I made myself this little chart to start to identify how far away I am and how many steps I took to get myself there and what I need to do in order to RETURN to the center.

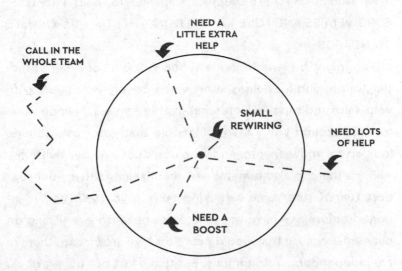

Sometimes I go all the way to the CALL-IN-THE-WHOLE-TEAM zone. Call the family, call the mentor, call the best friend, call the girlfriend, call the herbalist, call the sponsor, call in to a meeting, go to a meeting, call the therapist, make the infusion, and be RADICALLY HONEST ABOUT HOW BAD IT HURTS. And I can do all of this in about five hours.

With most addiction and distraction habits, I want so badly to make them go away BY MYSELF. I want to handle it Olivia Pope–style, but honestly, even she needs her team. So I am grateful to be inching back toward center! It takes being really, really honest about how low I get and being willing to take suggestions. And the next time I get away from my center, I know there are tools to bring me back, and that's something that will happen over and over and over again until I die.

THE FASTEST WAY I RETURN IS TO PRAY TO THE UNI-VERSE FOR HELP AND TO BE ABLE TO ASK FOR HELP AND TO STAY TAPPED INTO MY DAILY COMMITMENTS, AND THE SELF-FORGIVENESS AND LOVE WHEN I DON'T MEET MY IMPOSSIBLE STANDARDS.

You might be wondering how this is a part of a faith prac-tice, but asking for help is intertwined deeply with faith. With help, faith and trust feel interchangeable to me. It is imperative to build around you a team of people that you trust, admire, look up to, and lean into, and who don't cosign your bullshit.

Something to also remember is that having faith in your sup-port team is the same as having faith in yourself. As I men-tioned before, we have this innate desire to do everything on our own. Because that would prove that we are strong, that we are independent, autonomous. But that's just not how it goes. That is not the way to be strong. Plus, the only way we CAN ever handle anything on our own is to have the whole team. A lot of the time just the inherent knowledge that the team is there carries me through. I don't have to spin out all the way— just knowing I am not alone is of great benefit,

o   o   o

FAITH IN OUTSIDE MODALITIES

I have faith in different modalities that help me see through discomfort and better into myself.

For me, these include:

o Human Design
o Source Point Therapy
o Astrology
o Craniosacral Therapy
o Talk Therapy

These are things that bring me back to myself. They are things I seek out because, to put it simply: they make me feel better. And feeling better doesn't usually begin with feeling better, which also calls for extreme faith in the process. It takes looking deep within, which is usually very uncomfortable at first.

WHAT IF YOU are completely tapped out of faith? There's nothing left? Everything has proven there is no center and you can't get back, and you'll never get back and there's absolutely no way to find yourself and your joy or contentment ever again.

Welcome, you made it. Where so many of us have gone separately and together. And you aren't alone. If all you manage to muster is the deep knowledge that you are not the only one who has ever felt what you feel, then you will win. You will be okay. It might take a while if you've spun all the way outside the lines. But faith is about building the helper team back up.

Back to the point where you can grab a line and a thread that can pull you back.

In my own path of healing, remembering, getting to my center—as soon as I have decided that I am the only one who has ever fucked up, felt pain, experienced grief, unmanageability, I'm in trouble. I have put a fence between me and the universe, and instead of building a little door to walk through I now have to either run really fast to hop over or dig myself a hole to go underneath.

Let's see what we can do to restore our faith in the name of loneliness. In the name of isolation, abandonment, let us come back to ourselves.

Sort of like how I don't relate to the *you are enough* phrase, I also recoil at YOU ARE NOT ALONE. When I am sitting in my bed and can't stop crying and am spinning out and I read some yoga meme that says, YOU ARE NOT ALONE . . . What in the HELL? Are you seeing this? How much more LITERALLY ALONE could I be right now? I am completely and totally alone and no one is answering their phone and I am single, and I don't trust anyone all of a sudden. I AM ALONE.

Well, yes. You are. You're all by yourself. Maybe that's the difference. Alone versus being by yourself. But, in this aloneness, in this BY-YOURSELF-NESS, you are completely held by a web of humans, spirits, angels, deities, ancestors, who are holding you. Holding every limb, every broken heartstring, ever sore muscle, every question to the universe.

Have faith in this—have faith in the holding. In your own becoming, in knowing that in utter despair comes more holding.

You know that poem/story/laminated wallet card FOOT-STEPS? A man always sees his and Jesus's footprints in the sand and Jesus tells him, "I'll always be with you." But when the man is super sad and having a hard time, he is angry at Jesus. "Only my footsteps are there! HOW COULD YOU?!" And Jesus says, "No, no, I was CARRYING YOUR SAD-ASS BAREFOOT SELF THROUGH THE SAND CUZ U WERE SO SAD." Basically, *I got you, bro.*

It's like that. FAITH IS LIKE THE FOOTPRINTS LAMINATED WALLET CARD. It is your chance to lean into the divine mystery, the holy trinity that you invent.

I once invented a holy trinity that was Madonna, Janet Jackson, and my grandmother Marlys. Two of the three are living, so it was more like who is my little team I could call in if I really needed to. I add my grandmother Alice to this team, my grandfathers, Mortimer and Eldon, my uncle Brian—the people of my bloodline who aren't here but teach me about plants and deer and making blankets and money and joy and rest. If I have enough faith to find stillness, I can hear them.

You can invent whatever you want. Have I told you that yet? Magic is whatever you want it to be. Whatever you so desire. Magic is rocks and sticks and an altar of knickknacks you decide are important or not important and you pray to them and you ask for help and you carry on.

Another reminder to me that when I am spinning out into the darkness is the prayer of St. Francis, patron saint of animals and the environment, as far away from my center as I can possibly go, being of service to others and integrating selfless unconditional love can be the faith that serves and saves me.

god/goddess/divine spirit/universe: make me a channel of Thy peace; that where there is hatred, I may bring love; that where there is wrong, I may bring the spirit of forgiveness; that where there is discord, I may bring harmony; that where there is error, I may bring truth; that where there is doubt, I may bring faith; that where there is despair, I may bring hope; that where there are shadows, I may bring light. that where there is sadness, I may bring joy. Grant that I may seek rather to comfort, than to be comforted; to understand, than to be understood; to love, than to be loved. For it is by self-forgetting, that one finds. It is by forgiving, that one is forgiven. It is by dying, that one awakens to Eternal Life. Amen.

Theologian, comedian, and mover Riot Mueller taught me that at the end of St. Francis's life he had a robe that was tattered and covered in patches, and when his students offered to get him a new robe he said, "No, I want my insides to match my outsides."

May your whole life be a quilt of faith. Filled with imperfections and patched holes. May you delight in the ways that the patchwork of your life has sharp and curved angles, embroidered edges, and mismatched patterns. May it be unique and worn in, and may it be a light to all who desire their own perfectly imperfect quilt of a life. Accepting that you are loved and worthy just as you are, just as you are becoming: that is how we get to center.

IN CLOSING

This book, like all things, will come to an end. And you have reached it. This is the part where the pink clouds meet the blue sky in perfect holy matrimony to usher you out.

First of all, I want to say thank you. Going on the journey alone would have been worthwhile, but I don't believe it would have been as much fun. Even though I don't actually sit with you while you go through and read the pages, I am with you as you cross the finish line of re-centering.

Sometimes when we cross finish lines, though, it still kind of sucks. We're left with this feeling of: *Am I any different now? Am I better? Am I a winner? Did I even place in my age bracket?!* This is not the point, though. And when we started, I promised you that this book could not fix you. What it hopefully did, though, is give you a new window into yourself. It was the window washer to your pain, and it provided a sense of clarity to what is blocking you from your truest, brightest life.

This is what I want for you, so badly. I want for you to not feel small anymore, for you to shine so bright, for the people who don't want that for you to fall away. I want you to be surrounded by people who see you and love you for exactly who you are—which includes harms done, mistakes made, failures had.

I want you to go forth into the world with this new information, and I want you to transform the people around you with your joy and vulnerability. I want you to let grief wash over you so that you may be reborn over and over again. I want you to build the canoe to take your people to the other side of the river.

I pray for your imposter syndrome to fall away, for ease to fill your days, and for discomfort to be accepted one day at a time—in all its mystery in pain.

I pray you find glory and magic in every small thing, that you turn gratitude into action, that generosity becomes your way of living.

And most of all I pray that you keep your center. That you get to it. And then you get to it again. Over and over until you die. Because that is what being alive is: remembering and re-centering.

There is no right way to do this, and there is no timeline to short or too long. You are right on time. You can begin today. And if you fuck it all up, you can start over at any time. I promise to keep doing the same.

the one thing that is always true no matter what year or what day is that i promise to love so bright and be so alive that it beams back into the earth and the water and into the everything

Easy Does It
Marlee

ACKNOWLEDGMENTS

All my gratitude goes to:

To Kate Woodrow, my most consistent book-making team-mate, who helped me vision this concept from the very beginning.

To Emma Brodie, who received this book in its first incarnation and made a container for me to be my most vulnerable self.

To Elle Keck, who stepped up to edit this book and guide me through self-doubt and make it make sense.

To John Hanson, for being my family and letting me tell our story.

A conceptual thank-you to Alex Elle, who first introduced the word "harmony" to me as a replacement for "balance."

Fariha, for being the first person to read this book, for trusting me with your experience on Earth, for believing in me and helping to shape this book into what our Capricorn sun and moon knew it could be.

To John M. in the big meeting in the sky, for teaching me that my higher power could be a blade of grass.

To Jackie, thank you for loving me through this process, for being my witness in love and life, for boundless partnership, for holding your boundaries, and for celebrating my shadows instead of running from them.

The following people deeply impacted my life while I worked on this book; just being around them, receiving guidance from them, or texting with them has been a gift, and I am so grateful to each of them: Dori Midnight, Jacqueline Suskin, Jade Marks, Sarah Gottesdiener, Taylor Schilling, Emily Ritz, Ellen Rutt, Emily Sprague, Andrew Maguire, Lukaza Branfman-Verissimo, Jamila Reddy, Will Owen, Atiya Jones, Ariel Frey, Chloe Sells, Maceo Paisely, Whit Forrester, Owyn Ruck, Damian Mccan, Tatiana Godoy, Jenna Wortham, Jen Pastillof, Pam Vitaz, Robyn Kanner, Brandi Harper, Jacki Warren, Lola Kirke, Izzy Johnson, V Koski-Karrell, Jo the dog, Carl Solether, Megan Touhey, Chelsea Granger, Jake Kmiecik, Bill Lennox, Bobby Colombo, Megan Touhey, Wholesome House, Cindy Pincus.

To my students, newsletter readers, social media followers, book readers: thank you for learning alongside of me, thank you for the countless messages of encouragement and love.

To my New Mexico friend family, Beth Hill, Bett Williams, and Stella Linder Byrne.

My beautiful parents Bertz and Keeks, for being an example of partnership that can change and still be made of love, and to Sam and Kate—my sibling and his love—you remind me how to keep it light and have fun, to pay attention to plants and songs.

To Anna and my ladies who lunch crew as well as my St Stephens fellows—I couldn't have finished this book without your love and silent clapping over my computer screen.

To my dance teachers: Katherine Ferrier, Jennifer Kayle,

Pamela Vail, Lisa Gonzalez, Kathy Couch, Amy Chavasse, and Robin Wilson.

And to my true true, Katie Crutchfield, my soul mate in everything, I wrote this for us.

ABOUT THE AUTHOR

MARLEE GRACE is a dancer and writer whose work focuses on the self, distraction, creativity, and art making. Her practice is rooted in improvisation as a compositional form that takes shape in movement videos, books, online courses, and hosting artists. You can find her zines, things she makes, artists she hosts, and more at marleegrace.space/home.

As an author and workshop facilitator of dance and creative practice, which she has taught to groups across the country, she delights in the process of showing up to her own practice of being human, and finds great joy navigating it with others.